CLASSIC

FORD F-SERIES

PICKUP TRUCKS

1948–1956

DON BUNN

MBI Publishing Company

First published in 1998 by MBI Publishing Company, 729 Prospect Avenue, PO Box 1, Osceola, WI 54020-0001 USA

MBI Publishing Company books are also available at discounts in bulk quantity for industrial or sales-promotional use. For details write to Special Sales Manager at Motorbooks International Wholesalers & Distributors, 729 Prospect Avenue, Osceola, WI 54020-0001 USA. Library of Congress Cataloging-in-Publication Data

Bunn, Don.
   Classic Ford F-series pickup trucks: 1948-1956/Don Bunn.
      p. cm.
   Includes index.

ISBN 0-7603-0483-1 (pbk.: alk. paper)
   1. Ford trucks—History.
   2. Pickup trucks—History.
TL230.5.F57B86   1998
629.223'2—dc21   98-34963

On the front cover: Except for a few minor changes, Ford's 1950 F-Series trucks looked identical to the 1948 and 1949 models. The main differences included color choices and the relocation of the shift lever, which was moved from the floor to the steering column.

On the frontispiece: The standard grille on the 1950 F-Series was painted Argent, but, as in previous years, chrome continued to be offered as an option. The same was true of the bumpers, with black paint being standard and chrome an option.

On the title page: Ford introduced its 1951 trucks on Dec. 10, 1950, claiming more than 180 models available. These were really nothing more than variations on the F-1 through F-8 models that took into account engine and trim combinations.

On the back cover: Whether they're restored or modified, Ford trucks from the 1950s attract a lot of attention. The red 1956 model has been lovingly restored to its original condition; the customized 1953 pickup reflects the owner's personal tastes.

Edited by Anne T. McKenna
Designed by Tom Heffron

Printed in Singapore through PH Productions Pte Ltd.

CONTENTS

Writing a book takes an abundance of time—time away from other interests and especially from family. Fortunately, my wife Dinah and son Robert are very kind. They allow me to take the time to do what I have to do. I am most thankful for their generosity and understanding.

One cannot write a book without help. I am deeply indebted to Dan Kirchner of the American Automobile Manufacturers Association and to Mark Patrick, curator of the Detroit Public Library's National Automobile History Collection for reference materials. Another contributor who freely helped with his extensive knowledge of the F-1 and F-100 Series Ford trucks is Bill Wasner, a life-long, dedicated, and knowledgeable Ford enthusiast.

—Don Bunn

When Ford's management team met in 1947 to develop a long-term strategy to wrest the industry's truck leadership position away from Chevrolet, it is doubtful whether a single man at that meeting could foresee the importance light-duty trucks would play in future years. In 1947 total truck sales (all trucks, from lights to heavies) were 21.7 percent of the total automotive industry sales.

After two complete months of sales in 1998, pickups (full-size and compacts) captured 36.2 percent of the automotive market. (This number does not include vans and sport utility vehicles.) Total light-truck sales took 47.2 percent of the market in the same two month period. The same figure one year earlier was 46.3 percent. Truck sales gained .5 percent market share while cars declined almost nine percent! Full-size pickup sales slowed slightly in 1997, yet the annual growth rate has exceeded 10 percent in three of the previous five years.

No one foresaw that the full-size pickup market would nearly double from one million units a year in 1991 to more than 1.85 million in 1996. This increase was caused by a major shift in the economy in the early 1990s, which radically changed the way many people earned a living. More than one million start-up businesses a year reflected a trend of entrepreneurs—people creating their own jobs. In turn, this increase in new small businesses created a big demand for pickups and vans, many in the one-ton class.

Today, after 50 years of production, the F-Series is the all-time best-selling vehicle in the world, with more than 26 million in use. The F-Series has outdistanced the Model T and the Volkswagen Beetle, selling three-quarters of a million trucks in the 1997 model year alone.

When I decided to write this book, I specifically chose to include only the 1948-56 F-Series models. Collectors consider these years to be the classic era of Ford truck design. The book includes historical pictures and recently photographed truck restorations, an identification guide, production figures, specifications, and a narrative on the basic history of the development of this truck line. I also interviewed the people who planned, engineered, designed, and built the trucks to get the inside story—what it was like in the beginning. I wanted to make certain the book would include both the details that collectors crave and the interesting stories from people involved with the early F-Series.

I talked to one owner of a beautifully restored 1952 F-1 model, purchased new by his father in early 1953. He was one of 12 kids and the first eight learned to drive in the F-1. His story is not uncommon. Most F-Series owners are quite attached to their vehicles, believing their trucks are more than just mere transportation. They love their trucks.

The focus of this book is primarily on light trucks. However, the full F-Series line-up is included in the charts and mentioned throughout because of its importance to Ford in the postwar years. Although the Fords during that period were consistent in look and mechanicals, smaller details sometimes changed. For instance, different prices are listed for these early models because prices often changed monthly as the vehicles and economy changed. Other details (such as which paint colors were offered each year) varied, suggesting that these too may have changed depending on the plant of assembly and the time of year.

So keep in mind that the facts and figures of Ford trucks, or any other brands for that matter, can't be neatly categorized and placed in boxes. Many details changed on any given day, but then that's what kept it interesting!

I think you will enjoy reading about this wonderful era of original F-Series trucks and viewing original photos as well as the beautifully restored models. The F-Series Ford trucks are truly a part of the postwar American manufacturing and transportation history and the beginning of the best-selling vehicle line in history.

CHAPTER 1

1948 F-SERIES

The decade after World War II held promise of a booming economy, because few products had been available to the public during the war. People were ready to relax, spend some money, and raise their standard of living. During these postwar years, Ford was still expected to provide a good, solid value for the money to middle-class Americans. However, because General Motors had been using more modern business practices for years and changing their product line-up more often, Ford faced a serious challenge. Ford needed to be more productive and bring out some truly new vehicles—and quickly.

In 1945 Ford Motor Company was struggling to get domestic vehicle production rolling again. The company faced several problems, including the questionable leadership of Harry Bennett and outdated truck and car line-ups. Meanwhile, General Motors rose to No. 1 in truck sales, while Ford was clearly out of the competition. The company kept solvent only through several government contracts. Ford desperately needed a boost. Luckily, help was on the way.

Henry Ford II, the Leader

Henry Ford II became the executive vice president of Ford Motor Company in 1944. By September 1945, he was named president. His first act as president was to oust Bennett from the company. By 1946 Henry assembled the "Whiz Kids," a group of 10 ex-military brains, to help reform every area of the company. In one of his wisest moves, Henry II lured Bendix Corporation chief Ernie Breech to Ford. Breech had reorganized Bendix (a GM-owned company) and made it profitable. His position at Ford was executive vice president and general manager. Henry hoped Breech could bring some of his organizational magic to Ford as well. Apparently, Henry had the right

Although the 1948 models had a short list of options, such as a chrome grille, many owners added other items to make the trucks more attractive or more useful. This F-1 model has vertical markers on the front bumper, cab-top lights, and bumper-mounted fog lamps.

idea. By September 1947, Breech embarked on a modern new line-up of cars to be ready for Ford dealers by 1949.

A new range of trucks was already scheduled to debut in 1948. This fresh group of light, medium, and heavy trucks was the first of five decades of F-Series trucks, which were positioned as a well-built value for the customer. Over the years, the marketing strategies have changed, but customer value has always been a core focus. Even today, the "Ford Tough" marketing line strives to pitch an image of durability at a fair price—the "value" story.

For the 1948 models, Ford management wanted to create an all-new truck series with a modern, exciting look. If the buyer was going to get a truck with major improvements underneath, why not have a good looking body as well? So the design department set out to break away from the old-style, fender-mounted headlamps (last used in 1941), outdated vertical grilles, and all the other pre-war styles that would separate the old from the new. Chevrolet came out with the new "smiling grille" line-up the summer before, and was already outselling Ford by a wide margin. It was essential that the new Ford truck series catch the public eye and find a way into their hearts, or better yet, their pocket books. If the new truck series was successful, it would help put the company in a better financial position, as employees worked day and night to bring the 1949 model cars in on time.

Building a Team

Before the war, Ford's design, marketing and sales, and engineering departments designed and built vehicles without having much interaction. In most cases, one division would simply hand off the project to the next. In 1947, Ford management decided they needed a better plan. So, the product planning department was formed to build a more coordinated effort among the divisions.

Young Chase Morsey, only with Ford for about six months, remembers the early days in product planning with his teammates, working 14 hour days, six and seven days a week.

"I started working for Ford with the finance staff," Morsey says. "When we started Ford Division in 1948, L. D. Crusoe was vice president and general manager [Ford Division], and I was head of product planning. Prior to that time, engineering would tell the company what they were going to make and marketing and sales didn't have much to say about it. My job under Crusoe was to get engineering, manufacturing, purchasing and sales together. We coordinated all those groups. Before, they were all separate."

Don Petersen, later the chairman of Ford, was also a member of the truck product planning team during the late 1940s—according to Morsey.

Morsey recalls how Ford almost dropped the V-8 engine from both the car and truck programs for 1948 and 1949. "They gave me the [product] book for the 1949 Ford car, which had just been approved the week before. It just had a six-cylinder—they were dropping the V-8! I was just a young guy at Ford, but I said, 'Jack, this will break the damn company. The V-8 is the Ford car. I've owned Fords all my life and I know what a Ford ought to have in it.'

"So Jack said, 'OK, let's go in to see Mr. Crusoe,' and Crusoe said, 'How long have you been in the business?' I said, 'Six months, sir.' Crusoe asked, 'So you're going to tell me after my 30 years in the business and all of Mr. Breech's experience that you think you know more than us?' I said, 'Mr. Crusoe, I have one thing that all you guys don't have.

I was always a Ford owner, I love Ford cars and I know what makes a Ford go.' So he said, 'OK, I'll go see Mr. Breech but he'll be mad as hell.'"

Apparently, Ernie Breech was mad as hell, but he gave the product planning team 90 days to prove their case on the V-8. "We didn't have a marketing research department or anything, but we surveyed Ford, Chevy, and other owners to get the information we needed. The whole thing was done strictly by competitive analysis. The company had never really done anything like that before," says Morsey.

Ford was already in financial trouble, and without the 1949 Ford V-8, they might have been taken down. "When I went to work for Ford, they were losing a million dollars a day," says Morsey. "The same thing happened with the trucks. They wanted to just put a six in it—no V-8. Finance controlled the company and said that it cost $100 more to make the V-8 than the six."

Crusoe sent Morsey to see Roy Hurley in engineering. "They were coming up with automatic transfer machines so you could grind cylinders automatically without the manual labor. We proved we could make a V-8 within $16 of the six-cylinder and get $100 more for the model." The presentation to the board took two hours. "Ernie said he had been in many board meetings at General Motors," says Morsey, "but he had never been in one like that before. And he said, 'I move to keep the V-8 engine in the Ford cars and trucks.'"

The Coca-Cola Company of Atlanta, Georgia, used Ford products extensively in the late 1940s. This F-5 Series truck was fitted with a custom transport box with lockable side panels. Coke used various truck chassis sizes depending on the job at hand. *The Coca-Cola Company*

The Ford F-1 was by far the most popular selling model in the series. It could be used by small businesses or for basic farm work, doubling as a general transportation vehicle when not engaged in hauling a payload. This 1948 Ford public relations photo shows an F-1 being loaded with metal castings. *Ford Motor Company*

Marketing was still trying to compete against Chevrolet by pushing the six-cylinder engine in their advertising. They reasoned if market-leader Chevrolet sold only six-cylinder powered trucks, so should Ford. However, the dealers tended to push the V-8s, which made up a huge portion of the sales and ultimately helped Ford's V-8s become a sales success. It was a brilliant example of teamwork—product planning and finance working together to get the right product out the door. "Checks and balances. We respected them and they respected us when we proved our case," said Morsey.

Selling the Truck

The marketing team decided that "Bonus Built" would be the theme for the new 1948 models, proclaiming that Ford trucks offered more value for the money than the competition. The theme also built upon Ford's two-year-old theme "Ford Trucks Last Longer." The ads and dealer

brochures shouted to the reader, "Extra Thrift! Extra Reliability! Extra Durability!" for the F-2 series, while the F-1 was the "Master of 1,001 light delivery jobs!" The strategy was to provide the public with a great looking truck and improved technology at a better price than the competition, thus tackling Chevy head-on. Taking the sales lead was foremost in Ford's mind, even though Chevrolet still had a commanding lead.

Ford went all out to produce internal sales literature, customer sales materials, and sales tools for their dealer sales personnel. The company developed a detailed pocket guide to selling the new 1948 line-up of trucks. This added attention was unusual because trucks were considered somewhat of a necessary nuisance; the margin of profits wasn't nearly as lucrative as with cars. Only farmers and companies bought trucks, usually with very few options.

This was the first series of trucks that showed signs of having a more broad appeal because of the bigger cab, good looks, and a choice of engines. From the ads to the billboards, there was no doubt the company was claiming value and toughness for the customer. The features said it all. There were three new engines, a "Million Dollar" truck cab (with living room comfort!), Big Jobs (extra-heavy duty), a wide range of models, and many advancements throughout.

The 1948 salesman's guide (printed March 25, 1948) was distributed to dealers with the intention of stirring up Ford's national sales force.

The company was ready to put fire into the salesmen and move some trucks. The introduction started, "Right now Ford Truck salesmen are confronted with opportunities of unprecedented stature. The Ford Truck line is the hottest line in the business." It went on to describe the trucks: "Appearance-wise, Fords are the handsomest, truckiest-looking trucks on the road. Mechanically, they are all that a truck salesman ever wanted them to be . . . Three brand new engines! (What a terrific story you have here.) A brand new cab with new roominess, new seats, new ventilation, and chock-full of selling points that pack plenty of appeal for owner-drivers."

The salesman's handbook enticed them with the possibility of making big money. "Bigger Commission Checks! It puts you in on more deals than ever before." Ford pushed the new Big Job extra-heavy-duty line-up, because there was more profit in the heavy models. ". . . if you sell the special bodies and equipment that usually go with heavy trucks, you've got yourself into the big time folding green." There was no doubt Ford wanted salesmen to understand they could make a good living selling trucks, which wasn't always true in the past. The creative writers who wrote the handbook for Ford really turned on the heat. "You've got a smash hit sales idea which has within itself all the potency and chain-reaction qualities of atomic power. You've got a sales idea that competitors would give their collective right arms for . . . but which

The advertising theme for the new line of trucks was "Bonus Built," implying that you would get a strong, quality truck for a reasonable price. This ad shows the F-8 series cab pulling an impressive load. The art work commissioned by Ford was exceptional. The ads were created by the J. Walter Thompson agency. *Ford Motor Company*

they can't buy for love or money."

The last section of the sales guide, titled "Loaded for Bear," ended by saying: "It's up to you to get the Bonus Built sales idea across . . . but fast! What is important, is that the Bonus Built story, and all that goes with it, does a constructive job of building tomorrow's sales today in order to gain our objective of leadership in truck sales!"

When the first trucks hit the showroom floors on January 16, 1947, Ford probably never guessed just how big the truck business would finally become. Chevrolet would outsell Ford for many years, but Ford would ultimately take leadership for good.

Job #1—A New Era

Harry Truman defeated Thomas Dewey for president in 1948, and life was looking up for Americans as memories of World War II started to fade. The economy was beginning to boom and people wanted new cars to drive and new trucks for their farms and businesses.

Chevrolet, Ford, Dodge, and International Harvester all jumped at the chance to build something different than their pre-war truck designs. Chevrolet took the sales lead with a new model in dealerships by mid-1947, while Ford was moving about six months behind. But by November, Ford was ready to start rolling their new model trucks off the assembly lines in many plants across the country. Neither Dodge nor International posed a threat to the duo back then, each selling anywhere from 80,000 units on down to the 40,000 range in light trucks.

In the April 1948 Ford Atlanta plant employee newspaper, a detailed article described the first F-Series truck rolling off the assembly line the previous December.

The First F-Series Iron

The Atlanta plant was Ford's new gem and the first new plant since the war. But it wasn't actually the site of the

Ford Makes History Again As First Truck Rolls Off Line

History was made by the Ford Motor Company again on December 3, 1947, as the first unit rolled off the line here at the Atlanta Assembly Plant.

For several days before the first unit, a 114-inch light-duty truck with pickup box, came off the line there was a tension in the air, not only among those along the line, but throughout the plant. Everyone was anxious to see the new 1948 Ford truck.

J.B. Howard, superintendent of production, spent every minute of the day conversing with, and instructing, the men as the unit moved along the line. Enthusiasms ran high as the pilot unit gradually took shape and was nearing completion.

As the truck reached the end of the assembly line, at mid afternoon, on Wednesday, December 3, H.D. Lawson, superintendent of chassis and final assembly department, handed the keys to Henry C. Dorsey, plant manager. Dorsey climbed into the cab of the Arabian Green truck and after giving the motor a few turns, drove the first unit from the line.

A great feeling of pride was evident in the faces of all those present who had had anything whatsoever to do with the building of this product. Many were Fordmen of long years experience who had returned to the Company in the new plant, to pick up where they had left off when the old Atlanta branch was closed down at the beginning of World War II. This was indeed another history-making event in their Ford careers. They had grown with Ford since the days of the Model T and now they were witnessing the beginning of a new era—a new product was rolling off the assembly line in Ford's newest and most modern assembly plant.

The first 1948 Ford truck produced at the Atlanta assembly plant was delivered to Adamson Motor Company in Birmingham, Alabama, on December 19, 1947. It was sold by this dealer to the Metalplate Company of Birmingham on February 3, 1948.

The men turned immediately to the business at hand—that of building new Ford trucks. They had seen a sample of their handiwork driven from the end of the line and knew that the big job of producing many similar trucks and cars was one which they could handle skillfully and rapidly.

Four working days later, December 10, President Henry Ford II, accompanied by members of the policy committee, came to Atlanta to formally dedicate the new plant. There before them, in the plant parking area, stood 43 completed 1948 trucks and still more were coming down the line. The skeleton crew of employees at that time working in the plant was "going to town."

December 31 saw 351 trucks completed. By quitting time on January 15, the eve of the first public showing of this new Ford product, a total of 698 units had been completed in the new Atlanta plant.

When peak production is reached, 350 Ford trucks and passenger cars will be completed each day.

Forty-six railroad cars can be placed inside the new Atlanta plant walls for loading and unloading operations. At peak production 40 carloads of parts and materials will be required each day.

initial production F-Series. The first trucks came off the line at both the Highland Park, Michigan, and Richmond, California, plants November 27, 1947, a week earlier than Atlanta. The Richmond plant is often confused with Richmond, Virginia. Other than Norfolk, there was no Ford plant in Virginia. The Richmond plant produced vehicles until it closed in 1955 and production moved to San Jose, California.

Highland Park was the only dedicated Ford truck plant at that time. All other plants built light trucks and cars, which helped with distribution costs and kept the dealers in stock with a varied line of vehicles. Initially the F-Series trucks were built at 16 plants in North America (15 in the United States and one in Windsor, Canada). The transportation system in the late 1940s wasn't quite what it is today, therefore building regionally was important. It wasn't until much later that Ford dedicated certain plants to specialize in specific models.

F-Series—The Full Line

The new F-Series line offered a full range of trucks, from the F-1 1/2-ton light truck to the F-8 "Big Job" with a gross vehicle weight (GVW) of 21,500 pounds. The F-1 was known as the "pickup." The F-2 and bigger models, outfitted with a box bed (standard light pickup bed), were considered "express" trucks. The range included panel, pickup, express, stake, and platform bodies. The conventional models were available with either a 95-horsepower six, or an L-head (flathead) V-8 producing 100 horsepower. Cab-over-engine models (COE) were offered only in the F-5 and F-6 series.

The wide variety of models was designed to appeal to eager new customers across the United States. At the time many Americans were looking for a new car or truck with a little panache. And traditional truck buyers, while they were especially value conscious, appreciated getting a little extra style for the same price. The war years were all about sacrifice, so customers were ready for some "extras." While Chevrolet's design was new, Ford's design was revolutionary. The F-1 model was stylish and much more comfortable than most trucks of the past.

F-1 Series 1/2-ton trucks were built on a 114-inch wheelbase chassis and carried a GVW rating of 4,700 pounds. Models available included a chassis with cowl, chassis with windshield cowl, chassis with cab, pickup, panel, Deluxe delivery (panel), stake, and platform. The Deluxe delivery was not ready at the same time as the rest of the models; they followed four months later. The Deluxe delivery included the following extra equipment: Chrome-plated moldings on the hood sides, cowl, body sides, and on each rear fender; chrome bumpers, front and rear; two-tone paint; a cowl-mounted rear-view mirror; two-tone vinyl driver's seat; passenger-side windshield wiper; and chrome grille bars. The Deluxe delivery sold for $1,367. That was $60 more than the Standard panel. The retail price of the pickup was $1,144 when powered by the six-cylinder engine.

F-2 Series 3/4-ton trucks were built on a 122-inch wheelbase chassis and carried a maximum GVW rating of 5,700 pounds. Models offered included a chassis with cowl, chassis with windshield cowl, chassis with cab, pickup, stake, and platform. The retail price of the pickup was $1,287 when powered by the six-cylinder engine.

F-3 Series 3/4-ton heavy-duty trucks were built on a 122-inch wheelbase chassis and carried a maximum GVW rating of 6,800 pounds. Models offered included a chassis with cowl, chassis with windshield cowl, chassis with cab, pickup, stake, and platform. The retail price of the pickup was $1,379 when powered by the six-cylinder engine.

F-4 Series one-ton trucks were built on a 134-inch wheelbase chassis and carried a maximum GVW rating of 7,500 pounds with single rear wheels, and 10,000 pounds with dual rear wheels. Models offered included a chassis with cowl, chassis with windshield cowl, chassis with cab, stake, and platform. The retail price of the stake was $1,473 when powered by the six cylinder engine.

F-5 Series conventional cab 1 1/2-ton trucks were built on 134- and 158-inch wheelbase chassis and carried a maximum GVW rating of 14,000 pounds and 24,000 pounds as a tractor-trailer. Models offered included chassis with cowl, chassis with windshield cowl, chassis with cab, stake, and platform. The retail price of a 134-inch wheelbase stake was $1,487 when powered by the six-cylinder engine.

F-5 Series cab-over-engine 1 1/2-ton trucks were built on 110-, 134- and 158-inch wheelbase chassis and carried a maximum GVW rating of 14,000 pounds and 24,000 pounds as a tractor-trailer. Models offered on the 110- and 134-inch wheelbases included a chassis cab, stake, and plat-

Ford used watercolor illustrations for all the print ads used in their *Saturday Evening Post* layouts. Illustrations allowed for poetic license, leaving room for slight modifications to the proportions of the vehicles to make them look a little more streamlined than they really were. Notice this F-2 model had an upper-cab section that looks almost as if it were "chopped" like a hot rod. *Ford Motor Company*

form. The 110-inch wheelbase stake sold for $1,487 when powered by the six-cylinder engine. Only a chassis cab was offered on the 158-inch wheelbase model.

F-5 Series school buses (1 1/2-ton models) were built on 158-inch and 194-inch wheelbase chassis. Only a chassis with cowl model was offered, because the school bus body was built by another company, not Ford. The 158-inch wheelbase chassis with cowl sold for $1,240 retail when powered by the six-cylinder engine. Maximum GVW ratings were 12,000 pounds for the 158-inch wheelbase model and 15,000 pounds for the 194-inch wheelbase model.

F-6 Series conventional two-ton trucks were built on 134- and 158-inch wheelbases and carried a maximum GVW rating of 15,500 pounds and 28,000 pounds as a tractor-trailer. Models offered included a chassis with cowl, chassis with windshield cowl, chassis with cab, stake, and platform. The 134-inch stake model sold for $1,895 when powered by the six-cylinder engine.

F-6 Series cab-over-engine two-ton trucks were built on 110-, 134- and 158-inch wheelbase chassis and carried a maximum 16,000-pound GVW rating and 28,000-pound rating as a tractor-trailer. Models offered included a chassis with cab, stake, and platform. The 158-inch wheelbase model was offered only as a chassis with cab. The 110-inch stake sold for $2,055 when powered by the six-cylinder engine.

F-7 Series 2 1/2-ton conventional trucks were built on 135-, 159- and 195-inch wheelbase chassis and carried a maximum 19,000-pound GVW rating and 35,000-pound rating as a tractor-trailer. Models offered included a chassis with cowl, chassis with windshield cowl, and chassis with cab. The 135-inch chassis with cab sold for $2,670. A V-8 engine only was offered.

F-8 Series three-ton conventional trucks were built on 135-, 159- and 195-inch wheelbase chassis and carried a maximum 21,500-pound GVW rating and 39,000-pound rating as a tractor-trailer. Models offered included a chassis with cowl, chassis with windshield cowl, and chassis with cab. Ford's most expensive truck in 1948 was the 195-inch wheelbase F-8 chassis cab, which sold for $3,420 powered by a V-8 engine.

Light-duty models (F-1 through F-4) and medium-duty models (F-5 and F-6) were available with either a 226-ci, 95-horsepower inline six or a 239-ci, 100-horsepower V-8 engine. Both engines were L-head designs. The V-8 sold at retail for $20 more than the six in all models. Heavy-duty models (F7 and F-8) were powered only by the 337-ci L-head, 145-horsepower V-8 engine. The 337-ci V-8 was an adaptation of the Lincoln automobile engine.

One cab served the entire line from 1/2-ton to three-ton models.

F-1 Advertising Campaign

Although "Bonus Built" was the overall theme for the line-up, there were a number of advertising campaigns developed to deliver the value message to potential customers. The advertising was created by the J. Walter Thompson (JWT) agency, a business relationship that began in 1943. The company would develop a few basic ads and then Ford's marketing and sales team would choose the ones they liked. There wasn't a lot of strategy involved.

A series of full-page ads ran in the 1948 *Saturday Evening Post*, a favorite venue for truck advertising in the 1940s and 1950s. In each issue, the word "new" was stressed. Headlines included "New Clear Through!", "Brand Spanking New!", and "New, New, Brand New!" It

was important that this truck be presented to the public as a completely new vehicle in order to counter Chevy's fresh models, even though it shared many mechanical parts and the box bed of the 1947 model.

Besides the "newness" theme, advertising focused on economy, durability, and low cost of ownership. Ford used a tag line on most of their ads, saying "Life insurance experts prove and certify . . . Ford trucks last up to 19.6% longer!"

In the period directly after the war, customers wanted to feel like they were getting quality and strength—something they could use and count on for years. They wanted to be assured that if they invested their hard-earned money, they would have a product that would last.

Many of the ads had two license plates pictured at the bottom of the page. One said "Ford," and the other said "Trucks." On the left plate was "1948" and on the right was "1958," indicating that Ford trucks had a 10-year life expectancy. By today's standards, that might not be considered a big bragging point. But in 1948, 10 years was considered a long life for any work vehicle.

Above all else, Ford wanted to convince the customer that whatever their needs, Ford had the truck. Customer needs in the late 1940s included anything from hauling a cow to market to carrying monster-size concrete drain tiles for a road project. Ford print ads were colorful and portrayed the trucks in appropriate settings such as an F-5 on the ranch, an F-1 on the farm, a Big Job on a construction site, and a panel delivering to a department store. In each of these ads, extra features or bragging points were tacked on, including the "Million Dollar Cab", the "truck industry's first completely new engine line in years!", and "over 139 new models!" These ads were meant to show the public that Ford was back with

This F-1 panel truck picture gives the reader the idea that a Ford truck could be at home whether on a farm or in the city. This was the first time Ford tried pushing the idea that trucks could be more than transportation for a farmer. *Ford Motor Company*

a vengeance with a complete line-up that could handle any customer need.

The "Smart Idea" Campaign

One creative set of ads displaying the new Ford trucks was the "Smart Idea" campaign. Each one-page ad told a real-life story about a company that used Ford trucks to become successful. Ford assumed that everyone wanted to be a part of a success story.

A typical ad would begin by telling the story about a particular person's business. The lower half of the page exhibited photos of the owner with a Ford truck accompanied by text detailing the features that made Ford a better value. "You save money with the Ford Shiftoguide speedometer. It tells your drivers exactly when to shift transmission gears for best get-away performance with the least number of engine revolutions," read an ad for Youngblood's Fried Chicken in Texas.

Another ad featured restaurant owner Howard Johnson and his Ford trucks.

Smart Idea !—He built an ice cream cone into a chain of 230 roadside restaurants that gross $150 million.

Smart Move—He uses 40 Ford Bonus Built Trucks in his business! . . . Smart move! . . . Smart business!

Smart Bet—Howard Johnson's Smart Bet!

In this ad, one focus was on driver comfort: "Drivers keep cool in the Ford Million Dollar Cab with 3-way air control." The Million Dollar Cab included air-wing door glass and cowl ventilators as standard features. The optional Magic Air system was a fresh-air option. The ad went on to tell how once Mr. Johnson developed a chain of restaurants across the nation he used Ford trucks to haul ice cream.

Another unique "Smart Idea" ad showed Ford trucks hauling salt water creatures for Marine Studios in Florida. "We truck our sea world specimens from as far away as Key West," Douglas Burden told Ford dealer Pitt Barnes. "Our new 145-horsepower Ford F-8 Big Job is just the ticket for long runs like that."

The Million Dollar Cab

Features that helped sell the 1948 F-Series as an all-new, modern truck included the body design, engine line-up, and especially the Million Dollar Cab. The new cab, called "Million Dollar" for its roomy, modern feel as well as the company's design investment, was Ford's first effort at adding a little extra comfort to what had always been considered a workhorse segment of the market.

With the 1948 F-1 model, Ford promoted new features such as three-way air control and a coach-type seat for more comfort in a pickup than ever before. Extra space and driver amenities were the focus for the new cab

interior. "The Ford cab doors are wider," said one ad. "There's head room, too, and plenty of it in the Ford cab—one of the biggest in its class." Other comforts included a sun visor, ash tray, instruments that were larger and easier to read, and husky hardware. The ads boasted, "All these features encased in a weatherproof, all-steel structure designed to perpetuate the proved long-life superiority of Ford Trucks."

Ford's new "three-way air control" was a combination of air-wing ventilators, a cowl ventilator, and the optional "Magic Air" heater and defroster. The first two were self-explanatory—basically wing vents and a cowl scoop to force air into the cockpit. But Magic Air was a dealer-installed option. For an additional cost, this fan-and-heater unit pulled air in through the front grille, and used a hot water system from the vehicle's engine to provide warm air in the cab, similar to today's vehicle heater units. All three fresh-air sources were supposed to pressurize the cab to keep dust and cold air from coming in.

One unique interior feature for the new Ford truck series was the coach seat. This was a coil-spring bench seat, adjustable three inches fore and aft. The back could be inclined separately. It also raised to a higher position as it moved forward to accommodate the "short of stature."

Another option was the new Spiralounge Seat. This driver-side-only option was braced by a hinge from the rear of the seat to the floor while the weight was supported by a variable-rate spring, adjustable to suit the driver's weight. A hydraulic shock absorber, connected from the back of the cab to the back of the seat, helped control seat movement while the truck was in motion. The Spiralounge came standard only in the cab-over-engine models, but was optional in all others.

The cab itself was connected to the frame in a new manner, designed to insulate the driver. Rubber pads and rubber insulated bolts held the cab at the front corners. "Level Action" links in torsion-type rubber bushings at the rear corners were supposed to reduce noise, give a better ride, and prolong truck life. The driver-side windshield wiper was standard, but if you wanted a passenger-side wiper you had to shell out an additional $3. Of course the dealer only had to pay $2.25, leaving him with a whopping 75-cent profit.

Ford offered a number of options for dealer-only installation, providing dealers with an extra source of income. One of the reasons Ford promoted dealer-installed options when possible was that the buyer could often be talked into the options after buying the truck. The dealers certainly appreciated making the extra cash with the add-on options.

Truck Bed

There has been much speculation about the original materials used in the truck bed for the F-Series. Everything from all metal, to cedar wood materials in the original models has been suggested. But Ford used only hardwood sandwiched between stamped metal for the 1948-1950 beds. The hardwood sub-floor was put in place to keep the metal from denting as heavy items were thrown into the bed. The top and bottom surfaces were all metal with stamped-metal skid strips. Older models had strips that would work loose, but the runners on the 1948s were a part of the stamping.

The box was 49 inches wide, enough to handle the standard 4-foot-wide building materials such as drywall and plywood, and long enough to haul an average door. The box side panels featured a rolled-edge top, which strengthened the body and provided a better sliding surface for loading materials from the side. From 1948 to mid-1950, truck boxes had raised stampings on the sides framing the fenders. The 1951 models didn't have this bed side design. One feature unique to the 1948 models was black wheels on all models except the F-1, which had wheels matched to the body color.

Pricing

Ford priced the 1948 models aggressively in order to compete with General Motors and the new Chevrolets and GMCs, which had a six-month advantage out in the market. The retail price for a 1947 Ford light-duty pickup with a six-cylinder engine was $1,046. A new 1948 F-1 Series pickup was $1,144, a $98 increase. This was a great value, considering the difference in the two vehicles. But keep in mind that companies changed just about anything, including prices, at any time during those days. Although the Central Office in Dearborn released pricing in November 1947 for the 1948 models, the numbers likely changed several times during the model selling year. The new F-Series models were a big leap beyond the old Fords, but Chevrolet's sales were on a roll and Ford's marketing department had their job cut out for them.

Outlined below is a memo from the Ford Central Office to dealers dated December 18, 1947 indicating the pricing structure, options and standard equipment for the impending 1948 models:

MEMO
"FROM THE GENERAL OFFICE"

The following prices are effective November 24, 1947, for 1948 model Ford Bonus Built Trucks at the Dearborn Factory. Company's charges for distribution and delivery and all Federal, State and other Government taxes; also gasoline, oil and anti-freeze are extra (refer to General Information at the end of this letter).

1948 F-1 Series Trucks—1/2 TON - 114-inch W.B.

6 Cylinder		8 Cylinder		Models
Retail	Wholesale	Retail	Wholesale	
$ 890.00	$ 667.50	$ 910.00	$ 682.50	Chassis with cowl
920.00	690.00	940.00	705.00	Chassis w/Windshield Cowl
1,075.00	806.25	1,095.00	821.25	Chassis with Cab
1,144.00	858.00	1,164.00	873.00	Pickup
1,317.00	987.75	1,337.00	1,002.75	Panel
1,367.00	1,025.25	1,387.00	1,040.25	Deluxe Delivery
1,185.00	888.75	1,205.00	903.75	Stake
1,150.00	862.50	1,170.00	877.50	Platform

These prices include standard equipment including:

Air Cleaner—oil-bath type, one-quart capacity

Air Wing Ventilating Windows in doors of cab

Bumper —front-channel type; rear on panel

Clutch—10-inch diameter

Fenders, Rear-on pickup and panel, splash guards on stake and platform

Mirror, rear view—Inside on chassis-cab and pickup

    —Left, outside, short arm on panel

    —Left, outside, long arm on stake and platform

Oil Filter, replaceable element type

Running Boards—Long on pickup; medium on stake, platform and chassis cab, short on panel

Shock Absorbers —hydraulic double-acting telescopic, front and rear

Spare wheel carrier attached to frame at rear

Sun Visor—left side in cab, panel

Tail Light—right hand in addition to left hand on panel

Tires and wheels—five 6.00x16—four-ply tires, including spare.

Five wheels with 4 1/2 drop-center rims. Four hub caps

Transmission—three-speed

Windshield Wiper—left-hand, except on Chassis-Cowl

F-1 Series Options

Most of the real interest from the dealers came from the list of options for the new F-1 series, which was expected to be the big seller for the 1948 season. A right rear taillight and an eight-tube radio, for instance, were extra cost

F-1 Series Optional Equipment for Installation in Production

	Net Retail	Wholesale Price to dealer
Fan, heavy duty	$2.50	$1.88
Heater and defroster—recirculating type	36.00	27.00
Fresh air intake type	Price Later	
Radiator, heavy duty	5.00	3.75
Radio, eight-tube (except chassis-cowl)	Price Later	
Seat—Auxiliary for panel	32.50	24.38
Spiralounge for driver in cab types	7.50	5.63
Sponge rubber pad, full-width in Cab Standard seat cushion	15.00	11.25
Taillight, righthand (except Panel and Deluxe Delivery)	4.00	3.00
Tires—front, rear and spare (five tires) 6.00x16—six-ply	20.00	15.00
6.50x16—six-ply	35.00	26.25
Transmission, four-speed with 11-inch diameter clutch	25.00	18.75
Windshield wiper, righthand	3.00	2.25

The final page of the pricing document from the Ford Central Office to the dealers outlined general information about the new trucks that would be coming their way in January.

options. Above are the wholesale prices to dealers and retail prices to customers as printed from the General Office memo, November 1947.

General Information—F-1 Through F-8 Series Trucks Paint colors

Standard Colors
The following optional paint colors will be supplied at no extra cost:

Vermilion	Black
Arabian Green	Birch Gray
Chrome Yellow	

(Meadow Green replaced Arabian Green in the spring of 1948)

Wheels
Black standard, except F-1 Series which are supplied with wheels same as body.

Special Paint
Special color painting and art work will be supplied in accordance with the instructions and prices outlined in General Letter No. 33 (Sales-General) dated October 27, 1947.

Dealer Advertising
Amount shall be billed in accordance with district accounting department instructions.

Preparation and Conditioning
An amount of $20 per unit, designated as "Preparation and Conditioning," may be charged by the dealer.

Distribution and Delivery
Company's charges for distribution and delivery are outlined in General Letter No. 4 (Sales-Truck).

Gasoline, Oil and Anti-Freeze
Charges for these are outlined in General Letter No. 4 (Sales-Ford).

Federal Taxes
These shall be computed in accordance with accounting instructions, subject 15.3.

States of Texas and Missouri, and the District of Columbia
When advising dealers located in these named areas, include the following clause: "None of the prices set forth are intended to be determinative of prices on resales".

Optional Equipment
Prices shown in this letter are for items installed in production in lieu of standard and should not be confused with prices for the many new accessories for dealer installation as supplied by the Parts & Accessories Department.

Engine Power

The entry-level engine in 1948 consisted of an inline six known as the Rouge 226 (Ford 7HT). This powerplant produced 95 horsepower at 3,300 rpm. It had a much lower torque curve than the optional V-8, producing 180 foot-pounds at 1,200 rpm. With the standard 3.73 to one axle and a payload of 1,450 pounds, it could pull a 10-percent grade in high gear or a 30-percent grade in first. Although ads boasted engine speed at 35 miles per hour to be "an economical 1,600 rpm," it would be revving pretty high at today's highway speeds. And with the optional 4.27 to one gear, it became pretty much a farm machine with plenty of pulling power, but not built for running to town. In keeping with the advertising theme of durability and value, Ford pointed out that the Rouge 226 had new, longer four-ring Flightlight pistons to save oil, main, and connecting rod bearings that were replaceable, and series-flow cooling with thermostatic control that would allow exhaust valve-seat inserts to give longer wear. This inline six was promoted as "truck-designed, truck-built, from drafting board to final assembly."

The flathead Rouge 239 V-8 (Ford 8RT) was advertised to have a sizzling 100 horsepower at 3,800 rpm, but produced its 180 foot-pounds of torque at 1,200 rpm. This optional engine was equipped with a two-barrel carburetor. Both the 226 and the 239 engine blocks were painted red in keeping with the "Rouge" theme.

For the Big Job F-7 and F-8 models, Ford developed a truck version of the Lincoln 337 L-head V-8 called the Rouge 337 truck engine. It churned out 145 horsepower at 3,600 rpm and produced the expected killer torque rating of 255 foot-pounds at only 1,800 rpm.

All three engines used the Ford Loadamatic automatic-spark-advance ignition. The six was fitted with a single-barrel carburetor, while the V-8s used a two barrel. Only the 337 used hydraulic lifters. The Rouge 337 truck engine was an adaptation of the new flathead V-8, which became Lincoln's standard engine beginning with the 1949 model year. Formerly, Lincoln cars had been powered by a V-12 engine, which wasn't suitable for truck service. Ford truck engineers fitted the truck engine with stellite valves and a Holley Dual Concentric two-barrel carburetor with a governor. The truck engine's compression ratio was 6.4:1, versus the car's 7.0:1 compression ratio. Without the Rouge 337 engine, Ford would not have been able to enter the heavy-duty truck field at this time.

Vehicle Manuals

Driver's handbooks for the early models were detailed, educating the driver on everything from double clutching to setting the truck in motion. A 1948 manual describing double clutching said: "When shift-

"Brand New for '48" wasn't entirely correct. Although the cab was certainly new inside and out, most of the chassis and mechanical gear underneath were practically carryover equipment from the 1947 models. The flathead, or L-head six-cylinder and V-8 engines were also carryover, although substantial improvements had been made. *Ford Motor Company*

ing gears, it is advisable to double clutch. This is accomplished by halting the shift lever in the neutral position when shifting through the gear ranges and engaging the clutch while at the same time accelerating the engine to synchronize the transmission gears to the speed of the truck, then disengaging the clutch and completing the shift." It may have sounded a little complicated, but in 1948 a lot of people still knew how to double clutch.

By the end of 1948, Ford enjoyed a tremendous success, setting a new sales record of 289,971 trucks.

This was the best year since 1929, but still short of Chevrolet sales. The trucks provided the much needed income for Ford Motor Company as it readied the all-new 1949 sedans for dealer introduction.

F-Series Production Highlights
• On March 9, a second shift was added to the truck assembly line at the Highland Park, Michigan, plant. By the end of March, total employment on the line passed 1,100.

This 1948 F-5 stake-bed truck photo was probably taken in late 1947 prior to the dealer on-sale date of January 16, 1948. Notice the snow on the ground as men pose for the public relations photo. Quality may not have been comparable to today's vehicles, but it was a far cry better than it had ever been before 1948. *Ford Motor Company*

MIGHTY trucks for '48! *Bonus Built* to widen
Ford's Longer-Life Lead now up to 19.6%!

It's a proved fact! It's a certified fact! It's an unconsested fact that FORD TRUCKS LAST LONGER . . . up to 19.6% longer! And the new Ford Trucks for '48 are engineered to widen this longer-life lead. They're the strongest Ford Trucks ever built!

Look at the extra strength in the new Million Dollar cab . . . the comfort you can take for granted. New, exclusive Ford Level Action cab suspension prolongs cab life by eliminating cab distortion due to frame wear. The three new Ford Truck engines

have new performance, new economy, and new extra strength, too. Interesting example: porous-chrome plated top rings for pistons in the new 145 h.p. engine.

Extra strength all down the line . . . for the new BIG JOBS with G.V.W. ratings up to 21,500 lbs . . . for every one of over 139 new models. They're built with a strength never before attained in Ford Trucks. New strength! Extra strength! *Bonus Built* strength!

See your Ford Dealer! Get the facts on the strength engineered into Ford trucks for '48.

§ BONUS: "Something given in addition to what is usual or strictly due."—*Webster*

TRUCK INDUSTRY'S FIRST COMPLETELY NEW ENGINE LINE IN YEARS!

93 H.P. New Rouge 226 cu. in. SIX. 180 lbs.-ft. torque at 1200 r.p.m. 4-ring pistons. Precision-type replaceable main and connecting rod bearings. For all models except BIG JOBS.

100 H.P. New Rouge 239 cu. in. V-8. 180 lbs.-ft. torque. 4-ring pistons. Removable main and connecting rod bearings. Loadomatic ignition. For all models except BIG JOBS.

145 H.P. New Rouge 337 cu. in. V-8. 255 lbs.-ft. torque. 4-ring pistons, top ring porous-chrome plated. Hydraulic valve lifters. Hand-faced exhaust valves. For BIG JOBS only.

Listen to the Ford Theater, Sunday afternoons, NBC network. See your newspaper for time and station.

BUILT STRONGER TO LAST LONGER

. . . ENGINEERS ABOVE AND CERTIFY . . . FORD TRUCKS LAST UP TO 19.6% LONGER

An interesting tag line was used at the bottom of most Ford truck ads in the first few years of the F-Series. Two license plates—labeled "Ford" and "Trucks"—were shown with one plate dated 1948 and the other 1958. This, according to Ford, was approximately the life span of a Ford truck based on "insurance experts'" information. *Ford Motor Company*

- On June 24, Ford laid off 25,000 workers at the Rouge plant due to shortage of production parts. Ford's Kansas City assembly plant was also affected.
- Ford announced on July 7 a 5.4 percent to 9.3 percent price increase on its heavier truck models only.
- Supplier strikes, which began early in the year, continued to plague Ford as well as other truck manufacturers. A foundry strike, which began on June 19, halted output of Ford's medium-duty stakes on July 17.
- Ford boosted the hourly rate of 116,000 of its workers by 13 cents on July 12. Premium pay increases, vacation improvements, and group insurance plan changes were also part of the package.
- Ford and the United Auto Workers-Congress of Industrial Organizations (UAW-CIO) agreed on details of a new insurance program affecting 116,000 hourly workers on August 12.
- By August 14, Ford was in the process of building shipping-and-receiving docks at the Rouge plant's pressed-steel building to accommodate 65 trucks carrying 950 tons of material daily!
- The same day, Ford of Canada raised prices by $110 to $200 on passenger cars and truck models because of rising material and labor costs.

- Ford truck production was more than 1,600 units per day by the end of March. This represented the highest rate in Ford's history.

Grille Paint Procedures

1948—From the beginning of 1948 production to mid July, the grille was painted Tucson Tan with stainless steel grille bar moldings. From mid July to the end of 1948 production, the grille was painted aluminum (Argent) with two red stripes.

1949-1950—The grille was painted Argent.

1951, Early—The grilles of the Standard cab models were painted body color.
The grilles of the Deluxe cab models were painted Argent.

1951, Late—The grilles of the Standard and Deluxe models were painted ivory.

1952—The grilles of the Standard and Deluxe models were painted ivory.

1953—The grilles of the Standard and Deluxe models were painted ivory.

1954—The grilles of the Standard and Deluxe models were painted ivory.

1955—The grilles of the Standard and Deluxe models were painted off-white.

1956—The grilles of the Standard models were painted off-white. The grilles of the Deluxe models were chromed.

Engine Colors

1948-1951	Dark Red*
1952-1953	Medium Green
1954	Red
1955-1956	Pale Yellow

*Some late 1951s might have been painted Medium Green

Wheel Colors

All models came with black wheels, except the F-1, which had body-color wheels.

CHAPTER 2

1949 F-SERIES

In 1949 Ford truck sales reached 227,531 vehicles, but that was off the 1948 record mark of 289,971. However, on the car side, there was phenomenal increase in sales. Ford had added the modern-era 1949 sedan series, causing car sales to skyrocket. While 1948 only recorded sales of 305,761 cars, in 1949 the company sold almost 1.5 million cars. This provided a huge boost in capital to start immediate development of overhead-valve V-8 engines and new truck and car models that would be needed in the early 1950s.

F-1 Panel

The F-1 panel was a popular light-commercial vehicle for businesses from florist shops to plumbers. The bed was sealed tight to the side panels with weather-sealing strips to help exclude dust, fumes, and moisture. It was made of seasoned hardwood with metal runners for the floor surface. The standard driver's seat for the panel was a bucket-type unit that was described in company literature as comfortably cushioned, designed for proper driving posture, adjustable, and allowed easy access to the load area. A passenger seat cost about $32.50 and the now famous Spiralounge seat was available, only on the driver's side, for an additional $7.50. The Standard panel was almost $200 more than the base F-1 pickup.

F-1 Pickup

The F-1 pickup models continued to use a hardwood sub-floor, sandwiched between a metal outer surface with built-in, stamped-metal runners on the top layer. The 49-inch wide bed could easily hold standard 4-foot-wide building materials, and was long enough (6 1/2 feet) to

carry the average door. It had a capacity of 45 cubic feet. The side walls of the bed still had raised stampings for rigidity. The top edges of the bed sides were "rolled-edged flare boards" that, according to the dealer brochures, strengthened the body and offered a better sliding surface for objects loaded from the side. Of course, sliding materials over the flare boards wouldn't do much for the paint. In 1949, it wasn't exactly epoxy!

The tailgate was strengthened with a tapered truss-type rolled edge. The top edge was slightly thicker toward the center. If you looked closely from one edge to the other, it became obvious that this was done purposely to prevent the gate from bowing under heavy loads. Anti-rattle drop-chains helped to either hold the tailgate flush with the bed floor or let it swing all the way down.

Parcel Delivery Chassis

One new product, the parcel delivery chassis, was one of the few changes of consequence in the 1949 Ford line-up. As its name suggests, the parcel delivery was engineered for light and bulky loads only. This chassis was marketed in the F-3 series and was available on either the 104- or 122-inch wheelbase. Ford's parcel delivery did not include a body; customers purchased the chassis with front-end sheet metal, cowl, and windshield. The advantage of the parcel delivery vehicle was its huge cargo-carrying capacity, the ease of entry and exit for driver, and the many uses and jobs to which it could be adapted. Power came from the six-cylinder engine only; the maximum GVW was 7,800 pounds. An oddity with this truck was that it was equipped with the new heavy-duty three-speed transmission and a steering-column-mounted gearshift lever. Ford did not offer a steering-column-mounted gearshift lever as standard equipment on other light-duty trucks until mid-1950. Four parcel delivery chassis were completed at the end of the 1948 model year. In 1949, the first full year of parcel delivery production, Ford built a total for both models of 3,910.

The 1949 F-5 stake-bed model was still Ford's big-selling medium-duty truck. Note the standard black trim on the bumper, running boards, and wing vents. Obviously, the use of chrome trim was restrained. *Ford Motor Company*

Joie Chitwood, owner/producer of a well-known traveling thrill show, appeared in several ads for Ford, promoting his stable of 34 Fords, which consisted of 9 trucks and 25 cars. "This is the star of my troupe," said Chitwood of his F-8 car hauler. *American Automobile Manufacturers Association*

Special Bodies

Ford had agreements with many specialty body builders to modify F-3, F-4, or F-5 chassis trucks into special purpose vehicles.

Herman Body Company of St. Louis, Missouri, supplied the Herman Coldaire Body for milk deliveries to the home. The sales brochure read, "A complete package unit that eliminates the use of ice. Delivers milk in perfect condition at no increased cost to the Dairy or Consumer." The company claimed superiority in every way over previous cold-delivery vehicles, offering "Retail milk delivery bodies incorporating a new and different self-contained system of mechanical refrigeration." The system, based on modern air-conditioning, could maintain a temperature of 40 degrees and drain excess water away from the products and the vehicle. "Just start the motor and you have refrigeration." Herman Body sold its product conversions through Ford dealers, and told potential customers to "see your Ford dealer" in all its ads. Herman Body sold its trucks, F-3, F-4, or F-5, for $1,295. The company offered the following options:

Refrigerator-type rear door	
(30-inch opening)	$72.00
Mounting on dual wheel chassis	30.00
Dome light installed in load space	10.00
Windshield wiper on right side	15.00
Rear-vision mirror on right side	7.50
Painting—one color	48.00
Painting—two colors	67.50

Another important builder of retail milk-delivery bodies was the Schnabel Company of Pittsburgh. Schnabel built bodies for 1- and 1 1/2-ton chassis; 84-inch-long by 65-inch-wide bodies for the 1-ton chassis and 96-inch-long by 65-inch-wide bodies for 1 1/2-ton chassis. These bodies were built entirely of steel for a long, trouble-free life.

The McCabe-Powers Auto Body Co. of St. Louis, Missouri, was well known for their dependable utility bodies. They were all-steel construction and advertised as the ideal body for all types of general service utility work: electric, gas, water, street light, and telephone maintenance. Standard models were also available for plumbing, heating, and other service contractors. Compartment space and shelves could be arranged to fit the individual customer's requirements. Powers built models for 1/2-, 3/4-, and 1-ton chassis cabs.

Rockford Automotive Industries, Rockford, Illinois, built special bodies for 1/2-, 3/4-, and 1-ton pickups. One model, called the Rockford Panel Pick-Up Body, converted a conventional pickup body into an all-steel panel truck. The body was sold in a knocked-down form. It could be assembled and mounted to the pickup box in two hours. The firm supplied detailed installation instructions.

The *Ford Truck Times* was a publication produced from 1948 through the early 1950s as a companion to the *Ford Times*. It was primarily a magazine to promote new models and features, and to provide stories on real people and how they used their trucks. *Ford Motor Company*

Rockford also sold a dual-purpose Grain and Stock Pick-Up Body to fit every Ford pickup body. This body featured an all-steel grain box with removable, wood, stock-rack slats. The grain-tight box extended 36 inches above the pickup's floor, and featured a grain gate in place of the standard tailgate. The stock rack extended 2 feet above the grain box and was designed for hauling livestock. These units were also sold in a knocked-down package and could be assembled in two hours using the detailed instructions provided by Rockford.

The Oltman-O'Neill Co. of Detroit was an important manufacturer of all-steel, all-welded truck bodies. They specialized in van-type bodies for medium- and heavy-duty chassis cabs. The company's standard body offerings included 9-, 12-, 14-, and 16-foot lengths. They fit equally well on conventional or cab-over-engine models. Their standard model featured two X-braced, hinged, rear doors that folded flat against the body sides when fully opened. They also offered "Dutch" rear doors and special single or double side-opening doors. Costs of production were held down by modern assembly line methods of body building. All models were completely assembled, painted to match cab color, and mounted on the chassis at the factory.

Engines

The Rouge 226-ci six-cylinder engine was available in F-1 through F-6 models. It had four-ring Flight-light pistons to save oil, alloy exhaust valve seat inserts, a deep-breathing intake manifold for high efficiency, and

photo by Ray Manley

Traveling Salesman to the Navajo — a one-picture story

NELSON A. LINCOLN, driver of the pickup above, is one of the most popular travelers on the great Navajo reservation in northeastern Arizona. One reason is shown here: he and his companion are giving the oranges and candy they offer regularly to sugar-hungry Navajo children. Another reason is that Lincoln tours the reservation for Babbit's of Flagstaff, the Ford dealer, and one of the oldest trading firms in the Southwest. He takes orders from the Indians for merchandise ranging from horse collars, wagons, and flour to baby powder and velveteen for the women. The picture was taken near Harry Goulding's Monument Valley Post and Lodge, just over the Utah line. The formations in the background are the famous Mittens, 1200 feet tall. Lincoln found the children at play while tending their mothers' sheep and goats. ∎

Many of the Ford Truck Times stories were about a specific person and the truck was portrayed as a trusty, indispensable partner. The featured owner in this story was, ironically, named Nelson Lincoln. Ford Motor Company

Loadomatic spark control for more power and economy. The 226 was advertised as being able to pull a 1,440 pound payload up a 9.1-percent grade in high gear and the same load up a 30-percent grade in first with a 3.73:1 axle ratio. Using the optional 4.27:1 axle gave an advertised 20-percent increase in pulling power. Radiator capacity was 18 quarts, and the crankcase held 6 quarts of oil.

The Rouge 239-ci flathead V-8, the 8RT model, had a 6.8:1 compression ratio, a down-draft carburetor, and could run on gasoline with an octane rating of 72 to 74. This model produced 100 horsepower compared to the 95-horsepower six. The V-8 engine's radiator capacity was 23 quarts and the crankcase held 6 quarts of oil.

Mechanical Features

For 1949, Ford boasted fore-and-aft steering for greater stability and more uniform response under variable conditions. This engineering improvement supposedly provided better steering geometry and easier control. In reality, the trucks during this period had plenty of play in the wheel after a few thousand miles of driving when compared to the vehicles of today. But people seemed to learn to live with it, accepting this as the norm.

F-1 models were equipped with a semi-floating type Hypoid rear axle. It had forged manganese steel shafts, which were removable from wheel ends for servicing. Ford also promoted its removable brake drums, which "simplified maintenance." The drum could be bought separately for replacement.

Part of Ford's plan was to produce standardized parts to keep costs down and make it easy for owners to do much of the maintenance themselves. A dealer could be many miles away, so often much of the work was done either at home or at a local repair shop. Warranties were for only 90 days back then. Most owners figured if they could get the replacement brake drums or other parts, they could easily fix the truck themselves and save money. With Ford simplifying repairs, this made the F-Series a better buy for cost-conscious owners.

The Ford Truck Times

Ford always found many creative methods of promoting its cars and trucks. *Ford Times* and the *Ford Truck Times* were small-format magazines mailed to the homes of Ford owners and handed out at dealerships to prospective buyers. The publications were designed to be friendly, easy-reading magazines with stories about everyday Americans and their Ford cars and trucks. *Ford Truck Times* published stories about how owners used their trucks. Stories covered the range from light- to heavy-duty models. This bi-monthly magazine was also used as a means to alert the public to new models and features and to promote business for the dealers.

In the September-October 1949 issue, the lead article headline said, "New Bonus-Built Features Keep Ford Out Front." It read, "Introduction to the public of a new series of Ford trucks in no way means that a static period will exist until the next series is presented. On the contrary, Ford engineers keep up a steady flow of improvements which means a continuous expansion of the line. This has been the case in the 18 months since the current series was made available to the truck industry."

The article went on to cover details of the new options, announced by J. D. Ball, manager, truck and fleet sales, Ford Division. Most of the improvements dealt with the heavy-duty trucks, and included optional air brakes on the 21,000-pound GVW F-8, new exhaust valves on the 145-horsepower V-8 (Big Job only), and new camshaft and solid tappets. The big item for the F-1, F-2, and F-3 Series was the optional, heavy-duty three-speed transmission.

Smart Idea Advertising

Advertising in 1949 continued with the "Smart Idea" series, focusing on real-life stories of people using Ford trucks for business. Three-time champion race car driver Joie Chitwood used a fleet of 1949 Ford sedans for his traveling stunt-driving shows and a Big Job 145-horsepower

This Standard F-1 panel was used by a Michigan Florist for deliveries. *Ford Motor Company*

F-8 car hauler to carry the team's vehicles from city to city. The full-page October 12, 1949, *Saturday Evening Post* ad showed Chitwood's cars flying through the air, and Chitwood standing with a Ford dealer next to his F-8 big rig. "This is the star of my troupe," says Chitwood. "We expect a lot from our trucks like this 145-horsepower Ford Big Job, and we get it. We play Clearfield, Pa., one night, Faribault, Minn., 36 hours later. Ford trucks pull us through, on time, every time." Using well-known personalities such as Chitwood and photographing him with a dealer was Ford's way to bring a touch of reality to their ads.

Ford also collaborated with business partners such as Eaton Manufacturing, Cleveland, Ohio, for ad campaigns. Eaton ads in the *Post* pictured Ford F-8 trucks hauling huge loads of concrete drain tiles. "Heavy hauling costs less . . . With Eaton 2-speed axles!" In the ad, truck owner Max Schober says, "The Eatons save the engine and transmission. It shows up in our extremely low maintenance cost." The Eaton 2-speed axles provided double the ratios and could make life a lot easier on the drivetrain. Hauling heavy loads over thousands of miles could make this a cheap investment for many owners. Eaton ads portrayed real-life situations that the reader could identify with.

Almost all F-Series trucks were shipped with the standard black-wall tires, although the more fashionable whitewalls were an option. The wheels and gas filler cap and neck were painted black. *Ford Motor Company*

Ford truck sales for 1949 slipped to 227,531, down from 289,971 during a record year in 1948. But cars sales were up to more than 1.5 million, and business was looking good for the 1950s. *Ford Motor Company*

Dealer Options

Dealers continued to be an integral part of optional add-ons for the F-Series line-up. Magic Aire, the popular heater-defroster unit, was still available. This was the unit that "pressurized" the cab to "keep out chilly drafts and bring in fresh air." It used a thermostat control to regulate the heat coming into the cab, which also helped to keep windshield fogging down.

Radios were popular options for cars, but they were relatively new for trucks. The Ford custom radio, seven tubes plus rectifier, was a super-heterodyne receiver. The AM units could pick up local stations through the cowl-mounted antennae. The dealer-installed radio was mounted above the dash grille which came standard from the factory. The radio had four tonal ranges and push-button tuning.

Other accessories included a choice of seat covers—13-ounce nylon duck or a waterproofed fiber. Loud, trumpet-style, twin highway horns were optional accessories. If ordered, they were mounted between the grill and radiator,

to give a "pleasing" and louder blast from the horn button. Another popular dealer-installed option was a sealed-beam spotlight. Ford suggested this handy auxiliary light could be beneficial for finding road signs.

Engine governors were standard equipment on the F-7 and F-8 Big Jobs to keep engine speed down. They were optional equipment for medium-duty trucks. This was primarily of interest to fleet owners who wanted to keep their drivers from abusing the vehicles or breaking the speed limits.

Another option frequently seen on both the bigger trucks and the F-1 Series was a fire extinguisher. With late-1940s-style carburetors, fires could easily occur. If a fire occurred when a driver was out on the open road, miles away from help, the extinguisher could save the truck—and the driver.

Recapping the Year

Truck production in 1949 slipped from 1948, but overall the industry experienced a record year totaling

"QUICK THINKING AND FAST ACTION GOT ME $175 EXTRA ON A FORD TRUCK TRADE!"

"**W**hen I heard my Ford Dealer was making the best truck deals in town, I decided to check," says Andrew Ligeski.

"**It was a fact!** The offer looked extra good. And when I stopped to think that used truck values were slipping, and that I might take quite a loss if I waited, I made up my mind on the spot.

"**I'm tickled pink** I did. Used truck values have slipped so fast in the last three months, I figure my quick thinking and fast action got me at least $175 extra on a Ford Truck trade."

Your Ford Dealer invites you to listen to the Fred Allen Show, Sunday Evenings— NBC Network.
Listen to the Ford Theater, Friday Evenings—CBS Network. See your newspaper for time and station.

Ford Model F-1 Panel, one of over 150 models in the Ford Bonus Built Truck line for 1949.

GET THE HIGH-DOLLAR FOR YOUR OLD TRUCK
We've got the biggest monthly sales target of new trucks we've had in years, and we're ready to "deal". Phone us to arrange for an appraisal today.

IMMEDIATE DELIVERY!
We can make immediate delivery on many Ford Bonus Built Truck models. In fact, we can deliver most models "pre-war fast."

SEE US TODAY! SAVE MONEY!

BIGGEST TRADE-IN ALLOWANCES IN FORD TRUCK HISTORY

Ford had this ad produced for dealers to use in their local newspapers. This handsome gentleman was telling potential customers how he got a "quick $175 extra on a Ford truck trade!" Actually, the ad was somewhat misleading, suggesting that used truck values were dropping and that you could lose $175 by waiting three months to buy. *American Automobile Manufacturers Association*

This 1948 F-2 model is being given the "Coca-Cola" treatment in one of Coke's paint shops. Ford also offered special paint colors to companies as a factory option. *The Coca-Cola Company*

6,238,088 units of combined cars and trucks. The former production record was set 20 years earlier in 1929. As an indication of how good things were in 1949, the 1929 production record was broken by the end of October, whereas it had taken a full 12 months to set the 1929 record. Ford, GM, and Chrysler all debuted their first postwar automobile models in 1949, causing a great deal of excitement.

While production was astronomical, it would have been even higher if not for labor disputes. Ford was involved in one serious dispute. The UAW had targeted Ford out of the Big Three to dispute issues related to pensions and other fringe benefits. Another issue the union leaders considered critical was an alleged "speedup" in Ford's Rouge plant. A "speedup" occurred

when management increased the rate at which the assembly line moved past each workers' station. Plant productivity increased at the expense of workers' health and safety, according to union officials. Union leadership called a strike at the Rouge and Detroit Lincoln plants. Other plants were only able to continue for a few days. After losing 25 days of production, the strike was settled and production resumed on June 1.

For the first time since the war ended, the Big Three could purchase as much steel as they needed. That is, until the steel workers went on strike on October 1. The strike continued until early in November. In the end, the industry lost almost 400,000 cars and trucks to the steel strike. Even so, the year's total set an all-time industry record.

1950 F-SERIES

Happy days were back again for 1950 as sales reached an all-time record of 358,810 trucks, an increase of more than 130,00 compared to 1949. And with car sales of more than 1.5 million, the company was turning in strong profits. Ford wisely put much of the money back into research and development for future models.

Some of the money went toward developing new truck bodies for 1953 as well as the overhead-valve V-8 engine line coming in 1954. F-7 and F-8 Big Jobs had been powered by a modern OHV V-8 engine since 1952, while F-1 through F-5 trucks had a new OHV six-cylinder engine after 1952.

Ford had a number of new features and options to keep customers coming back. The company had a new Rouge 254-ci six-cylinder engine (model 8MTH) producing 110 horsepower available for the F-6 models, and full air brakes for the F-8 Big Jobs. Another option was the Synchro-silent four-speed transmission—a T98 Warner transmission. It was standard with the 254-ci, L-head six, and optional for all F-4 through F-6 Series trucks powered by the 226-ci, L-head six and the 239-ci V-8. The Synchro-silent was also offered for the F-3 Parcel Delivery model. However, it was not offered for the F-7 or F-8 Big Jobs.

Industrywide, truck production was well ahead of 1949, and almost equaling 1948's record. Light-duty models—specifically 1/2-ton trucks—were in the forefront, with sales increasing by 114,241 units. Two factors contributed to this increase. First, farming prospered and many farmers spent their income on new pickup trucks and other equipment. Secondly, the outbreak of war in Korea provided another impetus to light-duty sales.

Heavy-duty models surged ahead significantly after a slow sales year in 1949. Ford's truck production was the highest in August when 36,500 units were built.

Early industry predictions suggested a weak demand for trucks, yet sales grew unexpectedly stronger throughout the year. Ford and Chevrolet profited from labor troubles at Dodge Truck during the months of February, March, and April, followed by troubles at IHC from July through October. Demand for all types of trucks heavily taxed Ford's production capacity.

Cab Comfort

Historically pickups were not particularly profitable for dealers—mainly due to their lack of options. Farmers typically bought the trucks bare to the bone. If they wanted a heater, they may have the dealer add it later, or possibly pull one out of a wreck and hook it up under the dash. But times were changing as more people bought trucks. People wanted comfort and were willing to pay for it, if the options were available. The "Million Dollar" cab in the 1948-1950 models was certainly directed at driver comfort. Although trucks didn't offer the comfort level of a car, the 1950 models did offer a variety of heaters, dual windshield wipers, and radios. It might not seem quite like a "million dollars," but it wasn't bad compared to the old models.

The 1950 truck series had a movable driver's seat with two adjustments: a lever at the lefthand front corner for setting the seat backward or forward; and adjusting screws for tilting the seat back to the position best for the driver. COE models had an adjustment-screw knob on the lower left front of the seat. This wasn't exactly a quick way to move the seat every time a different driver got in the vehicle, but at least it was adjustable.

The floors were basically flat. They were covered by a rubberized floor mat that was easy to sweep clean or wash if muddy. Cab interiors in those days were notoriously drafty. It didn't matter so much during the warm months, but cold air drafts in winter were quite noticeable. Ford capitalized on this problem by pitching its Magic Air heating units.

The 1948 cab featured heavy posts at the four corners, which helped stiffen the entire truck substantially, but the posts were actually slightly narrower than the previous models. The smooth steel front bumper came standard and the rear bumper was an option.

"Pressurized . . . The new Ford truck Magic Air heater constantly circulates fresh air throughout the cab—warm in winter, refreshingly cool in summer." The unit pulled fresh air in through the radiator grille with a high-speed fan to build pressure in the cab. In theory enough pressure in the cab would force air out through the imperfections and the cold air would stay out. The same was true for dust.

The clutch, brake, and accelerator pedals were all floor-mounted. On the F-1 through F-3 models, the parking brake lever was located on the left side of the steering column, under the instrument panel. For the heavier models, it was located to the right of the floor-mounted gear shift lever. It looked like a second shifter.

Control knobs were located within easy reach, to make it more comfortable and safe for the driver. The gauges—including oil pressure, temperature, fuel and speedometer—were located directly in front of the driver. According to the operator's manual, "The various instruments and gauges provided are all located where they can be seen

quickly without taking your eyes from the road for more than an instant. Form the habit of observing these frequently to check the performance of your truck during operation."

The dashboard area around the gauges included control knobs for the windshield wiper, headlights (identified with the letter "L" on the knob), choke, cowl vent, and ignition switch. The foot button for controlling the low- and high-beam headlights was located on the floor to the left of the clutch. The beam indicator light was between the fuel and oil-pressure gauges. The wiper was vacuum operated. The more you turned the wiper control knob, the faster the wiper went.

The dash came standard with a radio grille. The radio and the speaker mounted behind the grille were dealer-installed options. Just to the right of the radio grille was the ash tray and the dispatch compartment, better known as the glove box in cars. At the top of the dash, on both sides, were defrost vents to direct warm air to a frozen or fogged

Ford was catering heavily to the commercial field by 1950, selling thousands of models like these F-5 models. Both the Rouge six and V-8 engines were capable of handling heavy loads and pulling this size of vehicle through rough terrain—which could be important to a company like Pennsylvania Power & Light. *Pennsylvania Power & Light*

Standard on the F-1 models were 6.00-16 six-ply tires; 6.50-16 or 7.50-16 tires were optional. The spare-tire carrier was located underneath the rear of the truck, starting with the 1948 models.

windshield. The speedometers on trucks with either four- or five-speed transmissions had a "Shift-o-Guide" dial to indicate the various speeds and corresponding shift points.

A Multitude of Models

Ford was now boasting more than 175 engine/model combinations. It had introduced the F-3 Parcel Delivery model, the new 254-ci six-cylinder, Synchro-Silent four-speed transmission, full air brakes on the F-8 Big Job, and the only V-8s in trucking. The F-1 through F-6 models came standard with the 226-ci six or the optional flathead 239-ci V-8. The F-7 and F-8 Series came standard with a 145-horsepower flathead V-8 based on the Lincoln engine.

Ford was still the only manufacturer to offer a choice of a V-8 or six-cylinder engine. The new, more powerful 254-ci six was available only in the F-6 models. It gave the drivers of medium-size commercial trucks the torque they needed in a six. The advertising read, "The new Rouge 254 makes the 1950 Ford F-6 the most powerful six-cylinder

This interior is from an F-1 Pickup, featuring a radio, a snap-in headliner, and a heater. The "Million Dollar cab" in the 1948-50 models was directed at driver comfort. Dealers offered a heavily promoted Magic Air heating unit, which forced air into the cab.

Meadow Green was one of the most popular colors on Ford trucks in 1948, second only to Vermilion. The painted area behind the headlamps and grille was available only in Argent gray.

The spare tire was conveniently located under the rear of the bed, between the frame rails, to save space in the bed. The standard rear axle had a 3.92:1 ratio and a 4.27:1 ratio was available for better pulling.

Ford offered a Rouge 226-ci inline six and a 239-ci V-8 in the F-1 through F-6 series. The Big Job F-7 and F-8 heavy trucks used the 145-horse-power, 337-ci engine derived from the Lincoln. All of the engines were L-heads, better known as flatheads.

A left-side taillamp was standard, but a right-side option was available. The tailgate was a heavy, stamped-steel panel with a truss-type rolled edge for stiffening. The center of the rolled edge was slightly thicker than the outer edges for added strength.

Warranties on the 1950 Ford trucks were only 90 days or 4,000 miles—whichever came first. Ford would ship the replacement part to the customer for installation, but would not pay for shipping.

Ford truck ever built." This engine was billed as having "free-turn exhaust valves, Autothermic pistons, chrome-plated top piston ring, high-lift camshaft, and many other power-producing, cost-saving, smart ideas." The Synchro-Silent transmission four-speed was standard with the Rouge 254 engine.

In 1950 only Ford offered V-8-powered trucks in their price category. The 100-horsepower 239-ci, L-head V-8 engine was offered in all light-duty and medium-duty trucks. It cranked out 180 foot-pounds of torque.

The 337-ci L-head V-8 engine, which powered F-7 and F-8 Big Jobs, produced 145 horsepower and 255 foot-pounds of torque.

Ford's L-head, 226-ci, 95-horsepower, six-cylinder engine with 180 foot-pounds of torque powered all light- and medium-duty trucks and F-5 cab-over-engine models.

Ford's other L-head six—the 254-ci, 110-horsepower engine with 212 foot-pounds of torque—powered only the F-6 cab-over-engine models.

The suspension was still a set of leaf springs, both at front and rear. Standard wheels for the F-1 were 16x4 1/2 inches and the tires were 6.00-16 four-ply rated. Six-ply rated tires were optional for heavier hauling.

Continued on page 43

The standard grille was still an Argent gray paint, but chrome continued to be offered as an option. The same was true of the bumpers, with black paint standard and chrome an option.

A long-neck mirror was optional for those needing better vision when pulling trailers or carrying bulky loads.

Standard and Optional Features

Standard features on 1950 model F-1:

6.00-16 four-ply rating tires (five)
three-speed transmission
10-inch clutch
3.92 rear axle ratio
oil-bath air cleaner
oil filter
double-acting shock absorbers, front and rear
front bumper
hub caps
tire carrier under frame
20-gallon fuel tank
driver-side sun visor
inside mirror
driver-side windshield wiper
long running boards
driver-side stoplight and taillight
jack and tool kit

Optional from the Factory:

11-inch heavy-duty clutch
4.27 rear axle ratio
heavy-duty fan
recirculating-type heater and defroster
fresh-air intake-type heater and defroster
heavy-duty radiator
sponge rubber pad for Standard cab seat cushion
passenger-side taillight
tires—6.00-16 six-ply rating in place of four-ply rating-tires
heavy-duty transmission—three-speed with 11-inch clutch
heavy-duty transmission—four-speed with 11-inch clutch
windshield wiper operational aids:
electro-vac kit (six-cylinder models)
fuel and vacuum booster pump (V-8 models)
passengerside windshield wiper

The center of the dash housed a chrome radio grille, which could be removed for a dealer installation of a radio and speaker. The ash tray was located just to the right of the grille, and on the far right was the glove box, described in the owner's manual as a "dispatch compartment."

The center bar of the lefthand louver also served as the hood-lock handle. The "F-O-R-D" block letters below the nose of the hood were common to the 1948-50 models. The first serious changes didn't come until 1951.

Whitewall tires were optional from the factory, but most customers purchased the trucks with the standard black-walls. Whitewalls were in vogue, but primarily to dress up cars.

Continued from page 39

90-Day Warranty

In 1950 warranties were only 90 days for new vehicles. This was not quite as reassuring as today's three-year agreements, but it was standard for the era. Below is the warranty stated in the Ford operator's manual.

Ford Motor Company Warranty:

The Ford Motor Company warrants all such parts of new automobiles, trucks and chassis, except tires, for a period of ninety (90) days from the date of original delivery to the purchaser of each new vehicle or before such vehicle has been driven 4,000 miles, whichever event shall first occur, as shall, under normal use and service, appear to it to have been defective in workmanship or material. This warranty shall be limited to shipment, to the purchaser without charge, except for transportation, of the part or parts intended to replace those acknowledged by the Ford Motor Company to be defective. The Ford Motor Company cannot, however, and does not accept any responsibility in connection with any of its automobiles, trucks or chassis when they have been altered outside of its own factories or branch plants. If the purchaser shall use or allow to be used in the automobile, truck or chassis, parts not made or supplied by the Ford Motor Company, then this warranty shall become void. This warranty is expressly in lieu of all other warranties expressed or implied and all other obligations or liabilities on the part of Ford Motor Company, and no person including any dealer, agent, or representative of the Ford Motor Company is authorized to make any representation or warranty concerning Ford Motor Company products on behalf of the Company except to refer purchasers to this warranty.

The Ford Motor Company reserves the right to make changes in the design and changes or improvements upon its products without imposing any obligation upon itself to install the same upon its products theretofore manufactured.

Basically, if the dealer and Ford decided that your part was faulty, you would get a new one and install it yourself.

One subtle difference in the mid-1950 models was the bed side-panels. In the 1948-49 models, the side sheet metal had a stamped, raised section. In mid-1950 the panels were flat.

1951 F-SERIES

Ford made a number of changes and improvements in 1951 F-Series trucks to increase economy, longevity, and to provide driver convenience and comfort. Highlights included engineering, styling, and safety improvements. There were four new truck engines, chassis changes, and the introduction of a new 5-Star Extra Cab. Only Ford offered buyers a choice of an economy six or a powerful V-8 engine to fit the buyer's power needs. The cab and front end were redesigned to give a more rugged and modern appearance. The rear window was redesigned and enlarged to more than 3 1/2 feet for full-range vision. The new instrument panel incorporated full-vision instruments, a rheostat-type instrument light switch, and a hand throttle on all conventional cab models. The weatherseal on the doors was improved, and the floor-pan area also was sealed against weather and fumes. Dual windshield wipers became standard equipment and were positioned to give a full-vision pattern on the one-piece windshield.

Improvements were most evident in the F-1. Performance of the F-1 light-duty models improved by changing the standard rear axle ratio from 3.73:1 to 3.92:1. The F-1's rugged, semi-floating rear axle with integral-type housing was standard. It featured removable shafts for easier inspection, adjustment, and maintenance. Big hydraulic brakes provided positive stopping control with easy pedal action. Removable brake drums simplified maintenance. Roll-Action steering reduced friction at three points for easier steering control. A stronger channel bumper attached directly to the frame for greater protection and more rigid frame support. Also new was a steering-column gearshift (actually new in mid-year 1950), with standard three-speed Synchro-Silent transmission,

Wheelbases for the F-6 were either 134, 158, or 176 inches. Weather-sealing on the doors was improved, and the floor pans were also sealed against weather and fumes from the engine.

for passenger-car ease of shifting.

The standard three-speed transmission for the F-1 was redesigned to handle more rugged loads, and to increase durability and shifting ease. It was synchronized in second and third gears.

F-1 Cargo Box

The F-1 pickup's cargo box was the industry standard 6 1/2 feet in length, 49 inches wide, and 20 1/4 inches deep. It provided 45 cubic feet of unobstructed load space. The cargo box had straight-sided corner pillars to assure a distortion-free body, and a wooden floor—protected by steel skid strips—replaced the former steel-floor bed. Payload capacity was 1,480 pounds. Maximum GVW rating for the F-1 pickup was 4,700 pounds. The 1/2-ton pickup rode on a 114-inch wheelbase chassis.

A sturdy, reinforced, level-opening tailgate was, "grain-tight" as a result of better fit between body sides and the floor. The tailgate when lowered was only 2-feet above the ground for easy loading. Rolled-edge flares provided for greater strength and better sliding surface when loading from the sides.

The most noticeable appearance change was in the grille, which was redesigned from the original five horizontal bars to a massive opening, which extended to the edges of both front fenders. A single horizontal bar spanned the grille opening, terminating at each end with headlights. Three upright Dagmars straddled the grille bar between the headlights. The front fenders were also redesigned to accommodate the wider grille. The large nostril vents formerly found on the front of the hood were deleted.

Seven paint colors were available: Vermilion, Raven Black, Meadow Green, Silvertone Gray, Sheridan Blue, Alpine Blue, and Sea Island Green. The Ford name was stamped into a chrome trim piece on the front of the hood, instead of mounted in block letters above the grille. A redesigned bumper was notched in the center for greater strength. The new bumper replaced the slightly curved channel-type unit that was formerly used.

Yet more changes were found inside the cab. A redesigned dash featured new instrumentation and a new radio grille. Two trim levels—5-Star or 5-Star Extra—became available. The standard 5-Star package included the features that had been found on Bonus Built Ford trucks since 1948: three-way ventilation, adjustable seat, dual windshield wipers, ashtray, dispatch box, and driver-side visor. The Deluxe 5-Star Extra package consisted of foam rubber padding on the bench seat; headlining backed by 1 1/2-inch glass-wool padding; additional sound deadener on the doors, floor, and rear cab panels; two extra chrome bars on the hood side trim; brightmetal for the windshield molding, vent window frames, and divider bar; Argent silver grille finish (on early units, later painted Ivory); two-tone seat upholstery, door panels, and body panels; two sun visors; armrests on both doors; a cigar lighter; door locks on each door; a locking glove compartment; a dome light; and twin horns.

Also new was a vacuum spark-advance mechanism called Power Pilot, which metered fuel and adjusted spark according to load conditions. Although simple in comparison to the computerized engine management systems on current trucks, Power Pilot was an early attempt to allow the burning of lower fuel grades and to automatically increase fuel economy based on the intake manifold's vacuum reading.

Continued on page 50

The bumper was attached directly to the frame to add rigidity. The grille came standard in ivory, and seven body colors were available including black, Sheridan Blue, Alpine Blue, Sea Island Green, Silvertone Gray, Meadow Green, and Vermilion.

Styling changes came with the 1951 models, but mostly in the form of trim modifications. The F-Series now came with a painted grille. It was advertised as ivory, but it came in silver (Argent gray) with the "5-Star Extra" cab option.

The Ford bed offered the lowest load height of any truck in its class—only 2 feet from the floor to the ground. The lowered tailgate was flush with the bed floor, so heavy merchandise could slide easily.

The new chrome identification piece in the nose of the hood was meant to give a new look to an aging body. The "F-O-R-D" name was stamped in chrome and a V-8 emblem was mounted just below the front of the hood if it had the optional 239 flathead.

A new automatic Power Pilot caburetion-ignition control was standard on all engines. It was supposed to provide power with economy by metering and firing the correct amount of fuel at the right instant under varying loads without spark knock.

Gas caps came either in chrome, with the 5-Star Extra cabs, or in body color on the rest of the lineup. The gas tank was still located behind the driver seat, and both doors came with locking cylinders.

Ford moved more than 70,000 of these F-6 models in 1951, many in stake-bed form. It was a popular, affordable medium-duty truck that could be used to haul just about anything. Dual windshield wipers were now standard.

Continued from page 46

F-2 3/4-Ton Pickup

The Ford F-2 Series 3/4-ton pickup carried a maximum GVW rating of 5,700 pounds. Its wheelbase of 122 inches carried an 8-foot cargo box with a 62 cubic-foot capacity. Buyers had a choice of the two new 5-Star cabs. The 3/4-ton had a big-capacity steel body for bulky loads. Its box was built with reinforced side panels and heavy corner posts with a rounded arch section for greater strength and rigidity. Payload capacity was a hefty 1,948 pounds. An interlocked sturdy wood floor, protected by steel skid strips, proved durable even for severe service. Anti-rattle locking chains closed the tailgate tight to prevent loose loads from spilling out.

1951 Ford F-Series Truck Line-up

Ford advertised an "All-Star" line-up of more than 180 models. Ford slotted these All-Stars in five general categories.

1. Light-duty models, F-1 through F-4
    F-1 1/2-ton models featured the following body types: pickup, panel, Deluxe panel, platform, and stake.
    F-2 3/4-ton models featured the following body types: pickup, platform, and stake.

The new dashboard incorporated full-vision instruments and a rheostat-type instrument light switch.

The 110-horsepower Big Six engine was popular in the medium-duty trucks because of its low-end torque for pulling heavy loads.

F-3 1-ton models featured the following body types: pickup, platform, and stake.

F-3 1-ton parcel delivery chassis on either 104- or 122-inch wheelbases.

F-4 heavy 1-ton chassis cab on a 134-inch wheelbase.

2. Heavy-duty models, F-5 and F-6

F-5 on three wheelbase lengths featured stake and platform bodies and chassis cabs.

F-6 on three wheelbase lengths featured stake and platform bodies and chassis cabs.

3. School bus models, F-5 and F-6

F-5 chassis cowl only on a 158-inch wheelbase.

F-6 chassis cowl only on a 194-inch wheelbase.

4. Heavy-duty cab-over-engine models F-5 and F-6

F-5 on three wheelbase lengths featured stake and platform bodies and chassis cabs.

F-6 on three wheelbase lengths featured stake and platform bodies and chassis cabs.

5. Extra heavy-duty models, F-7 and F-8

F-7 chassis cabs only on five wheelbase lengths.

F-8 chassis cabs only on five wheelbase lengths.

1951 Production Results

This was a very unusual year for the automotive industry. It was somewhat of a throwback to WW II with production controls being reinstituted for the first time since late in 1945. Added to production controls were spiraling labor costs, ceiling prices, materials controls, and a crippling railroad strike in February that nearly brought the automotive industry to its knees. Ceiling prices were the government's method of controlling inflation. Consumers had money to spend but goods were in short supply because much of America's production capacity was concentrating on war materials. The government was also concerned with a shortage of certain raw materials—

F-2 through F-8 models still came standard with a floor shifter, and the doors were painted the same as the body. Five-star cab amenities included were a cigar lighter, dispatch compartment lock, dome lamp with automatic door switches, and chrome hardware.

The grilles of the early 1951 Standard cab models were painted body color. The grilles of the Deluxe cab models were painted Argent. On late 1951 production, the grilles of the Standard and Deluxe models were painted ivory (shown).

The F-7 and F-8 Big Job trucks used the 337. Both models used a 12-inch clutch and 20-inch wheels. The tractor-trailer load ratings on the F-8 topped out at 41,000 pounds. *Ford Motor Company*

Early 1951 5-Star Extra cab models had silver trim in the grilles (shown). The 1951 trucks also had a channel steel bumper in the front and dual wipers standard. *Ford Motor Company*

such as copper, zinc, and chromium—which were vitally needed for producing defense materials, therefore, these materials were controlled.

Raw material shortages impacted automobile production significantly in 1951. The government tightly controlled access to nickel, which was a critical material used in bumpers, grilles, hub caps, wheel covers, instrument panels, gas caps, and interior and exterior trim. The shortage of copper affected the manufacturing of car heaters, radiators, and radios. Scrap metal was another important material in short supply. It was thought that

without scrap, the quality of steel needed for autos could not be produced.

In spite of these problems, the industry fared surprisingly well. Car production was down by 1.3 million units from 1950, but it was still the second-highest production year in history. Trucks, on the other hand, hit an all-time high exceeding 1.4 million units for the first time. A closer look at the numbers reveals some interesting facts. First, the two annual production leaders, Chevrolet and Ford, took hard hits because sales of light-duty trucks declined substantially. The government set up the

The 5-Star cabs featured 65-coil spring seats with two-way adjustments, Air Wing ventilators, and Level Action suspension. New weatherstripping was now installed to bolster the dust-tight design. The instrument panel was redesigned with a new radio grille and instrument layout. An important addition in the F-1 models was the first "three-on-the-tree" column shift.

This 1951 F-1 was used on the beaches of Florida. Note the modest bathing suits for the lifeguards! *Ford Motor Company*

National Production Authority (NPA) this year to control scarce materials in an attempt to assure the production of vehicles and other critical goods needed for the Korean War. This somewhat explains why car production decreased while truck production hit a record high. Dodge and Willys, truck manufacturers who built military trucks for the war, set production records. Ford and Chevrolet, who were the industry's usual leaders in light truck production, suffered declines. Ford did build more than 23,000 conventional chassis models, mediums, and heavies for the government in 1951.

Beginning in the third quarter, the government's NPA controlled critical manufacturing materials and allocated them to truck manufacturers on the basis of factory sales for the years 1947-1949, with an adjustment for sales during the first quarter of 1951. These material allotments allowed the industry to build a total of 256,000 trucks—139,637 light-duties, 83,780 medium-duties, and 32,583 heavy-duties. These were quotas for civilian trucks only. The government allowed manufacturers to build all government-ordered trucks in addition to their allotment.

Prior to the NPA cutbacks, truck production for the first two quarters of the year was the highest ever recorded. Ford's truck output reached its highest level from March through June, when daily production hit 1,500 units per day. Ford's second quarter (April-June) produced 95,809 trucks. If this pace could have been held for the remaining quarters, Ford would have had its best year ever by a wide margin. But this was not to be. For the year, about 57 percent of total Ford production was devoted to trucks rated at less than 10,000 pounds GVW. This result was consistent with the industry.

1952 F-SERIES

In 1952 the F-Series Ford trucks were at the end of their body-style run. The press was reporting the company would introduce all-new styling for the 1953 models, and the public could see the existing trucks were growing a bit long in the tooth. Total truck sales for 1952 declined, as did overall sales for Ford Motor Company.

The F-1 1/2-ton model production for the year was 108,006, more than one third of the total truck production of 289,971. The trucks were still providing good profits for Ford, especially since the tooling and engines had been around for several years and styling changes were limited to little more than a new grille.

Wheelbases were one way to differentiate between the F-1 and F-2 models. The F-1 had a 114-inch wheelbase and the F-2 had a 122-inch wheelbase. Both were available with a new overhead-valve six-cylinder (101-horsepower) or a V-8 (106-horsepower) engine. The price for the F-1 with the standard six engine was $1,329, an increase of $79 over the previous year. The price for the F-2 pickup with the standard six-cylinder engine was $1,494, an increase of $83 over 1951.

Styling Changes

F-Series truck styling was largely unchanged in 1952, another signal that this would be the last year for Ford's first new postwar truck series. The hood nose-vent molding was painted, the Ford nameplate was moved to the crossbar above the grille as on 1948-50 models, and the series emblem was placed in a round disc, forward on both sides of the hood. Engine choice was designated by either a V-8 or six insignia in the center of the hood nose molding.

Although basically the same as the 1951 models, the 1952 F-Series bodies had a few chrome and trim changes to the exterior. The trucks were made at 16 assembly plants in the United States and also at Windsor, Canada.

F-1 Panel

F-1 buyers were offered a selection of two handsome panels for 1952: the Standard panel and the 5-Star Extra panel at an additional cost. The 5-Star Extra cab included heavy Masonite lining on the interior panel sides. It also had acoustic headlining backed by a glass-wool insulating pad extending the length of the roof panel. The panel's reinforced steel body was welded together for greater strength. It contained 160.3 cubic feet of load space, and carried a payload up to 1,330 pounds. Weatherstripping was used throughout for a better seal against dust, fumes, and moisture. A spacious weather-sealed driver's compartment, with adjustable bucket-type driver's seat, offered more driving ease. Its loading height was only 2-feet above the ground.

New Engines

Even though the styling of the F-Series was largely unchanged, 1952 was a year of big changes for Ford trucks, especially in the engine category. First, an all-new, modern six-cylinder engine with overhead valves (the first for Ford trucks) replaced the former L-head six. Named the Cost Clipper Six, this engine had a cubic-inch displacement of 215.3 and produced 101 horsepower at 3,500 rpm. Its compression ratio was 7.0:1, and it put out 185 foot-pounds of torque at 1,300-1,700 rpm. Bore and stroke were 3.56x3.60. The new six was used in all trucks from F-1 through F-5 conventional trucks, to F-5 school bus chassis, and all parcel delivery chassis. The old flathead 254-ci "Big Six" engine was only used in the F-6 models. It would be two more years before Ford could re-engineer its world-famous 239-ci V-8 with overhead valves.

Ford's first modern overhead valve V-8 engine, the Lincoln 317, came in 1952 and was used, in various sizes, in the 1952 F-7 and F-8 Big Jobs. The F-7's engine had a cubic-inch displacement of 279, a horsepower rating of 145, and torque rating of 244 foot-pounds. The F-8 had a

The F-Series trucks came with a gear-and-ratchet-type jack for changing tires, although the jacks were generally used for about everything else around the farm as well. The beds were hardwood with metal runners for sliding the cargo.

neers specified the L-head V-8 for service in Series F-1 through F-6, including cab-over-engine models.

Heavy-Duty Big Six

Ford's L-head Big Six for 1952 developed 112 horsepower at 3,500 rpm from 254 cubic inches and a maximum torque of 217 foot-pounds at 1,400-1,700 rpm. The Big Six was the standard engine for Ford's popular F-6 and F-6 COE mid-range trucks. The Big Six, when installed in COEs, was equipped with an updraft carburetor and was rated at only 110 horsepower. It featured a cast-steel alloy crankshaft with seven counterweights for better balance and smoother performance. The high-lift camshaft resulted in quieter operation. Its top piston ring was chrome-plated to prevent scuffing during break-in and reduce long-term cylinder-bore wear. Heavy walled, replaceable main bearings were carefully chosen for closer tolerance. Full-pressure lubrication prolonged engine life.

F-6 Series Trucks

Ford's F-6 Series medium-duty two-ton trucks were very important to the company in 1952. To be precise, Ford referred to its medium trucks as heavy-duty models

cubic-inch displacement of 317.5 and a horsepower rating of 155 and 284 foot-pounds of torque. The F-7 engine was a down-sized version of the F-8 engine, which was a "built-for-truck-service" version of the new Lincoln engine.

Ford's tried-and-true 239-ci, L-head V-8 continued with only an increase in compression ratio to 6.8:1. Higher compression boosted horsepower to 106 at 3,500 rpm and raised maximum torque to 194 foot-pounds. Ford engi-

Ford was still promoting durability, using information from "insurance experts" in a survey to claim that Fords would outlast the competition. The entire truck line-up was advertised as a great value, which included quality, comfort, and economy.

The chrome trim on the side of the hood changed slightly from the previous year. The easiest way to identify the 1951 models from the 1952s was to look at the nose of the truck. The 1951 models had FORD stamped in the chrome piece on the nose of the hood. The 1952 models had FORD written in chrome block letters just above the grille, but not on the hood.

The gauges were a carryover from the previous year, and the starter button was still located on the lower-left side of the dash.

In a Ford efficiency move, the 1951-52 models used one gauge to include what was previously four in the 1948-50 models. This one includes the battery charge, fuel, oil pressure, and temperature.

A new 112-horsepower Big Six was offered in the F-6 models, while the F-1 (shown) through F-5 series had the Cost Cutter Six as the standard engine. A 106-horsepower flathead V-8 was optional in the F-1 through F-6 models.

and its heavy-duty models as extra-heavy-duty trucks. The F-6's importance to Ford is noted by the sales total of 62,728. The single biggest seller in the series, at 31,365 units sold, was the 158-inch wheelbase chassis cab. The F-6's maximum GVW rating was 16,000 pounds; maximum gross combination weight rating was 28,000 pounds.

Model availability included 9- and 12-foot stake and platform bodies; chassis with cab; with windshield and with cowl. The series consisted of both conventional cab and cab-over-engine models. COEs totaled only 5.6 percent (3,539 units) of the total production. Buyers had the choice of a 5-Star or a 5-Star Extra cab. There was also the choice of Ford's 106-horsepower V-8 or 112-horsepower Big Six engines. Three wheelbases in the conventional cab line, 134, 158, and 176 inches, provided a chassis length selection to accommodate special-purpose bodies. COE models came in three wheelbase lengths: 100, 134, and 158 inches.

The F-6 powered with the Big Six engine and equipped with a two-speed rear axle (at an extra cost) pulled its 16,000-pound gross load up a 5.7-percent grade in high. Level-road speed fully loaded was more than 55

miles per hour. The F-6 tractor pulling a 28,000-pound combination gross load could maintain a level-road speed of 47 miles per hour.

1952 Painting Specifications for Ford Trucks

There were seven standard 1952 colors available for all models except the school bus and parcel delivery chassis, which were furnished in primer only. The colors were Vermilion, Woodsmoke Gray, Glen Mist Green, Meadow Green, Sheridan Blue, Sandpiper Tan, and black.

The standard body colors were applied to the hood, fenders, cowl, cab, and body, including all interior metal surfaces of cabs and panel body before trimming. Body color was also applied to the wheels on F-1 Series and running boards on panel models. Cowl and cowl-windshield models were regularly painted in primer unless standard body colors were specified.

The center grille bar, the three supporting brackets, and the headlamp bodies were finished in a neutral Ivory paint, which accented any of the standard body colors. Grille assembly for school bus and parcel delivery chassis was furnished in prime only.

The frame, running boards (except panel models), outside rearview mirror, door divider bar, taillamp, wheels (except F-1 Series), springs, axles, fuel tank (if frame mounted), and bumper were painted black.

Door handles, windshield wiper arms and blades on all models, plus fuel tank filler caps on panels, were supplied in stainless steel.

All of the above specifications also applied to the 5-Star Extra and 5-Star Extra panel models. However, the vent window frame, door glass divider bar, and windshield reveal molding were finished in stainless steel. Inside Masonite trim and the floor of 5-Star Extra panel body were painted light gray.

New Courier Model

The only new model for 1952 was the Courier panel delivery, which was based on the beautiful styling of the new two-door Ford Ranch Wagon. The rear side windows were replaced by a large, blank area for a sign. Companies could display their name and logo in this area. The Courier's load space measured 6 1/2-feet long by 4 3/4-feet wide. Maximum GVW rating was 4,500 pounds. Ford offered both the new 215-ci OHV Cost Clipper Six, rated at 101 horsepower, and the venerable 239-ci, L-head V-8 engine, rated at 110 horsepower. There were three transmission options: a three-speed manual, three-speed with overdrive, and Fordomatic Drive. A brown vinyl bucket driver's seat with 4 1/2 inches of fore-and-aft adjustment was standard, along with a door armrest and sun visor. An optional passenger seat was offered.

The Courier's interior provided a total capacity of 102 cubic feet, with a load space 6 1/2-feet long to the back of the seat, 59 inches wide and 39.2 inches high. The Courier rode on a 115-inch wheelbase chassis. Maximum GVW rating was 4,500 pounds. Its wide rear door opened 44 1/2 inches at the floor. The rear door's check held the door open in a 90-degree position. The load area was built from a two-piece welded, steel floor pan with a plywood floor for long-lasting load protection. The body interior was lined floor-to-ceiling with fiberboard, and front to back with a woven fiber headlining. The Courier's cab interior sported a smart two-tone color scheme.

Since the Courier was built on a passenger car chassis, the driver enjoyed the handling ease and driver comfort of a passenger car. A delivery man could drive his route faster, with less fatigue, which meant more stops per day and more trips per week. The optional Fordomatic automatic drive also resulted in less driver fatigue. Ford built a total of 6,225 Couriers in 1952.

The dashboard remained basically unchanged. The clutch and brake pedals were still floor mounted.

The F-1 series came with either the Cost Clipper six-cylinder or the Rouge 239-ci flathead V-8 engine. The three-speed column shift was matched to the Synchro-silent transmission, synchronized in second and third gears.

Payload for the 1/2-ton F-1 express truck was up to 1,480 pounds with 45 cubic feet of cargo space. A rear bumper, righthand taillight, heater and defroster were all still optional.

F-1 5-Star Cab and 5-Star Extra Cabs

The 5-Star cab was designed and built to reduce driver fatigue and to make the driver's job easier, more efficient, and safer.

Highlights of the 5-Star Cab included:
- More visibility with a 50 percent bigger rear window and a full-vision one-piece windshield.

- More safety with Ford's all-welded steel cab and easy-to-read instruments.

- More convenience with wide doors for easy entrance and exit, handy back-of-seat storage, steering-column gearshift (F-1), two windshield wipers, a driver-side sun visor, handy ash tray, and dispatch box.

Highlights of the 5-Star Extra Cab included:
- Extra riding ease with soft foam rubber padding in full-width seat.

- Extra insulation including perforated acoustic head-lining, backed by a 1 1/2-inch glass-wool insulation pad. Sound deadener on door, floor, and rear cab panels.

- Extra looks: Stainless-steel windshield molding with brightmetal vent windows frames and door-glass division bars.

- Extra appointments: Two-tone seat upholstery, customized door and body panel trim. Bright metal hardware escutcheons.

- Extra conveniences: Two adjustable sun visors. Grip-type arm-rest on both doors. Illuminated cigar lighter. Two door locks. Sturdy lock on glove box. Dome light with automatic door switches. Twin, matched-tone trumpet horns.

Full Model Line-up

In 1952, Ford's truck line ran the gamut from the 114-inch wheelbase 1/2-ton F-1 series with a maximum GVW rating of 4,700 pounds to the 3-ton F-8 Big Job with four wheelbases up to 195 inches and maximum GVW ratings up to 22,000 pounds and 41,000 pounds as a tractor-trailer. Retail prices ranged from a low of $1,329 for the F-1 pickup to $3,834 for the F-8 Big Job chassis cab.

1952 Truck Retail Price Comparisons

	Dodge	Chevrolet	Ford	GMC	IHC
1/2-ton pickup	$1,509	$1,392	$1,445	$1,477	$1,568
1/2-ton panel	1,729	1,604	1,667	1,637	1,759
3/4-ton pickup	1,654	1,554	1,594	1,624	1,738
3/4-ton stake	1,726	1,627	1,668	1,696	1,823
1-ton pickup	1,751	1,677	1,702	1,750	1,854
1-ton stake	1,840	1,767	1,766	1,839	1,960
1 1/2-ton stake	2,219	1,864	1,950	2,070	N/A
2-ton stake	2,492	2,077	2,345	2,322	N/A

1952 Production

Total industry output for 1952 tumbled almost 15 percent to only 1,217,765 trucks total. Two problems accounted for the slowdown. First, the government again limited total auto and truck production because resources were conserved due to the Korean conflict. Next, a serious mid-year steel strike quickly dried up stocks, causing production to hit rock bottom from July to September.

Ford's 1952 production in the United States alone totaled only 236,753, a decrease of more than 80,000 units from 1951.

Ford's successful Bonus Built trucks series ended in 1952. Ford engineers and designers were busy preparing a fully re-engineered and redesigned truck line for 1953, which would prove to be one of the most popular truck designs of all time.

CHAPTER 6

1953 F-100 SERIES

Ford invested more than $50 million in research, development, engineering, testing, and dies and tools for the new 1953 truck line. It was the "revolutionary new approach" to design with a focus on the driver. "Every component affecting driver fatigue has been designed and engineered to make the driver's job simpler and less tiring and to permit him to get this job done faster," read a *Ford Rouge News* article on the new trucks.

By 1953 Ford had produced more than 17 million commercial vehicles in the United States alone, and claimed to have placed all of its experience and know-how into the new models. The Synchro-silent transmissions eliminated double clutching. Cabs had wider seats and broader rear windows, and a one-piece curved windshield provided 55 percent more visibility.

The *Ford Rouge News* was a good source of Ford history. It provided employees with coverage of everything that went on at the "mighty Rouge" and other local plants. The front page headline for the February 6, 1953, edition read, "Stamping Plant Begins Production of Body Cab Parts for Ford Trucks." January 26, 1953, was the date the first parts started rolling out of the Dearborn stamping plant. Prior to this date, truck body stampings had been made by outside vendors. This was an important move for Ford to be able to manufacture its own parts for production. The stamping site produced door, hood, and fender assemblies; back, floor, and roof panels; and upper and lower grille sections for most truck models. The plant used 79, multi-ton, mechanical punch presses for both truck and car parts.

Ford tested the new vehicles on over 300,000 miles of highways in various parts of the country before bringing them to market. The new F-100 models had a 110-inch wheelbase (shorter by 4 inches) and a wider track. The turning radius was shortened by 14 percent over the previous model.

The New Look

Some say it's the most handsome of all light trucks. Unquestionably distinctive, the Ford F-100 series truck with a tall cab, smartly slanted windshield and short roof represented a clean, modern look. Gone were the fat lines of the Bonus Built series. From every angle, the F-100 looked ready for action. This truck barely launched its hauling career when it became a favorite of the street rod set. Smart styling, yes, but what really set the F-100 apart was its driver appeal. "Hop in, let's head for the open road," the F-100 seems to beckon. There's no mistaking, this is a truck meant for driving. And that's part of the plan. For the first time in truck history, Ford engineers made the driver their most important consideration when designing the F-100 series. This extra attention paid off. Today the F-100 is among the most highly valued of all light trucks by serious truck collectors.

1953 F-100

Ford Motor Company celebrated its 50th anniversary in 1953. The car line, which was restyled in 1952, was one year old, causing the newly restyled for 1953 truck and farm equipment lines to hold the spotlight. The F-100 carried a family resemblance with the car line; no one would question that the new trucks were built by Ford. Yet the golden anniversary pickups represented a clean break in every department except for the engine choices. The trucks had a totally redesigned cab, and a grille opening that stretched to the outer edge of the front fenders. Ad writers bluntly called it a massive look. The 1953 Ford 1/2-ton pickups sported a longer (6 1/2-foot) and taller (20-inch) box which would be seen on Ford pickups into the 1980s. Keeping pace with the times, the pickup tailgate carried the Ford name in modern block letters—a stark contrast from the company's traditional script.

Ford trucks for 1953 were big news in the industry. With a curvaceous new body and redesigned interior, Ford truck sales rose from a total of 253,454 in 1952 to 280,895 in 1953. The F-100 model alone sold more than 133,000 units, up almost 39,000 from 1952.

Perhaps the feature that set the F-100 Series sharply apart from previous Ford trucks was the expansive window area. Windshield glass increased 55 percent and was curved on the new series rather than flat. For added visibility, the rear window was now a full 4 feet wide. A highly regarded feature of the new cab was its "armrest side windows." What this meant was that the extra side window glass resulted in lowering the truck's beltline and, consequently, the window ledge. Along with giving drivers and passengers greater side visibility, those responsible for boosting sales were quick to remind buyers that in a Ford truck you could enjoy that relaxing posture of resting an elbow on the window ledge while driving.

"Driver Engineered" is how Ford described the cab of its new truck. The accent here was on comfort—more

of it. Cab dimensions inside were stretched to 60.7 inches door-to-door with a seat-to-roof height of 36.1 inches. According to the ad claims, the new wider seat of 56.7 inches gave "roomy comfort for three men." In making their claim the ad writers weren't discriminating against women by using a man's posterior as a yardstick. As a sign of the times, in 1953 a woman was not commonly seen in a truck unless she was accompanying her husband to town.

However, women responded with great enthusiasm to the Deluxe version of Ford's new "Driverized" cab, the finest truck cab ever built! When Ford named its cab "Driverized," it meant that it was designed with the driver in mind. A slight extra cost gave buyers the following customized added benefits: foam rubber seat padding;

The tailgate for the first time had FORD block lettering across the back. The previous year had "Ford" in script. The bed was basically a carry-over, but with the new cab and front end, the truck took on a new look.

The graceful fenders and cab body lines attracted thousands of new buyers in 1953. The fuel tank was moved to just inside the frame rail under the cab, providing for storage space behind the seat back.

thermacoustic headlining backed by sound-absorbing glass-wool insulation; sound deadener on the floor and back panels; two-tone seat upholstery and interior trim; two sun visors; two arm rests; dome light with automatic door switches; lock on the dispatch box and both doors; twin electric horns; and appealing chrome or brightmetal hardware and exterior trim.

The modern, comfortable F-100 pickup was attractive to women who began riding and driving pickups. Among its departures with tradition, the F-100's seat upholstery wasn't the moose-nose-brown vinyl typically seen when opening a truck door. A simple but aesthetic amenity, the vinyl seat covering was given a touch of passenger car class by adding two color-coordinated bands—one across the front cushion, and another on the backrest. The chief of automotive writers, Tom McCahill, wrote about his F-100 road test in *Mechanics Illustrated* in October 1954, "Inside, the cab has a three-passenger bench seat which is as com-

This Deluxe model had the famous chrome teeth in the grille. These were only used with the Deluxe models. The engine line-up was primarily the same as 1952, but along with the new cab and interior was the first Ford truck automatic transmission, the Fordomatic.

The 1953 models moved away from the flat windshields and into the modern world of curved glass. The 1953 model had 55 percent more windshield area and swept-back pillar posts. The rear window grew from 3 feet to 4 feet wide.

fortable as the average sedan's. . ."

The newly styled instrument cluster also reflected a brush with car styling. Although plain in comparison with the garish instrument arrays in many 1950s cars which modeled the driver's controls after an aircraft cockpit, the F-100's small instrument pod grouped the speedometer and full set of gauges in front of the driver for easy visibility.

A redesigned ventilation system drew fresh air through a large cowl vent and a side cowl intake that ducted air to the heater and defroster. The vent wing windows also directed blasts of fresh air into the cab at the driver's discretion.

For 1953 light-duty Ford trucks retained the venerable 239-ci flathead V-8 and the 215-ci OHV six, which had been introduced in 1952. Despite the V-8's two-cylinder advantage, power ratings for the two engines were nearly the same with 106 horsepower for the V-8 and 101 horsepower for the six. It should be noted that the Canadian Mercury M-100 series, which was really a Ford truck by a different name, retained the old L-head six. In the United States, however, the improved breathing of the overhead

valve six gave economy-minded buyers nearly the performance of the V-8 with considerably better fuel mileage.

Transmissions

"The Greatest Transmission Choice in Truck History" was how the F-100 sales brochures introduced the four transmissions offered. In another driver-convenience first, a truck automatic transmission was included in the line-up. For 1953, the automatic was only available in the 1/2-ton models, however. Manual transmission choices included a Synchro-mesh three-speed, a three-speed with over-drive, and a four-speed. Ford had finally replaced the old crash-box transmissions and both the three- and four-speed gearboxes featured synchronizers in the upper gears for smooth, quiet shifting. Down-shifting into low gear still required double-clutching so as not to clash gears.

Actually, two three-speed transmissions were available: the standard gearbox supplied with the F-100, and a heavy-duty unit that was installed in the F-250 and F-350 models. The most noticeable difference between the standard and heavy-duty transmissions was the gear ratios. First gear on the F-100 three-speed gave a drive ratio of

The 239-ci flathead V-8 was in its last year and could be ordered with either an all-synchronized manual or the new Fordomatic transmissions. The 215-ci six produced 101 horsepower and the 239-ci still flexed 106 horsepower.

2.78:1. Trucks fitted with the heavy-duty gearbox crawled off the mark with a lower 3.71:1 first gear. A column-mounted shifter snapped both three-speed trannies through the gears. In the 1950s a column shift was considered a convenience feature for the driver and the center passenger. The four-speed gearbox used a floor shift and was a real stump-puller with a 6.40:1 first-gear ratio.

Along with the several transmission options, numerous rear-end gear ratios could be selected. When fitted with either the three-speed or four-speed transmissions, final drive ratios were either 3.92:1 or 4.27:1. When over-drive was added, available rear-end gearing was either 4.09 or 4.27:1. The automatic transmission was paired to a 3.92:1 rear-drive ratio. Still lower ratios were supplied with the F-250 and F-350 trucks.

Although the low rear-end ratios caused higher engine rpm at highway speeds, the 16-inch tires (retained through 1955) compensated somewhat for the steeper gearing. As would be expected, tire sizes increased with load capacity from the familiar 6.00x16 for the F-100 to 7.00x17 on the F-350 models.

New Model Designators

Among the changes for 1953, Ford overhauled the model designations for its truck line-up. The F-100 replaced the former F-1 identification on the 1/2-ton pickups. More substantial reshuffling occurred up the scale as the F-2 and F-3 models were combined into the new F-250. Although the F-250 received a shorter, 118-inch wheelbase than the former F-2 model, when fitted with oversize 7.50x17 8-ply tires, the new F-250's GVW rating was a substantial 6,900 pounds. Like the F-100, the heavier F-250 could be ordered either with a cargo box or stake-bed, though the F-250's express body was a full 8 feet and the stake bed measured 7 1/2-feet long. At the top of the light-truck scale, a new F-350 replaced the Ford F-4. With a wheelbase stretched to 130 inches, the F-350 was available with either a 9-foot stake-bed or an express body. Equipped with single rear tires, the F-350's GVW rating was 7,100 pounds. Duals at the rear made a 9,500-pound GVW.

Ford management's plan was to develop three new light truck models in a "stepping-stone" sequence, which allowed a wide range of customer options. By stretching the chassis and beefing-up such components as brakes and springs, plus adding heavier-duty tires, Ford actually arrived at five payload options and three cargo styles (express, stake or platform, and panel) in its three light-duty series. In addition,

The ivory-color paint on the grille complemented almost any color combination without clashing. This model was the lower line without the chrome teeth on either side of the center section.

The 1953 F-Series had the first push-button door handles on a Ford truck. It also had a one-piece curved windshield and a wider rear window. The frame was made of heavier deep-channel steel for a more rigid chassis. The F-Series now gave the driver better visibility and superior handling.

bare chassis and cowl, or cowl and windshield configurations could be ordered in each series for conversion to a variety of special uses.

Shorter Cab-to-Axle Dimensions

Another significant design change for 1953, but one that takes a sharp eye to spot, is the shorter cab-to-axle distance on Ford's new light trucks. It was a feature introduced on the B-series Dodges and later adopted by IHC on its L-series. Ford relocated the front axle 4 inches to the rear on the F-100 and larger series Ford light-trucks, reducing the turning radius and improving the weight distribution by shifting the load center forward.

Other usually unnoticed changes included relocating the gas tank under the left side of the frame from its earlier mounting inside the cab, and spreading the front axle tread to 60.55 inches. Gasoline filler caps on the F-100 and larger series are found on the left rear corner of the cab.

The new grille housed the V-8 emblem when equipped with the 239 flathead. The Six had the three-pointed star emblem.

The Ford truck crest made its debut on the 1953 model.

The 1953 line-up represented the 50th anniversary of Ford Motor Company, and all truck models came with the anniversary horn button. All the gauges and the speedometer were housed in one cluster in easy view of the driver.

The rear doors on the F-Series panel trucks were designed to stay open under most circumstances. They were also made to open at an acute angle and lay over toward the sides of the vehicle. The rear bumper was a $7.48 option.

Pickup Bodies

The taller, 6 1/2-foot-long cargo box on the F-100 models provided 45 cubic feet of enclosed cargo space. The box itself was assembled by a combination of rivets and bolts, which allowed relatively easy replacement of the side panels. Wooden planks continued to be used for the floor, with steel skid strips covering the joints between the

boards. As a benefit to drivers and passengers alike, as well as bystanders, 4-inch rubber cushions were positioned on each side of the tailgate to prevent rattles.

The express box on the larger F-250 and F-350 models was of bolted construction. Unlike the F-100 pickup box, which measured 49 inches between the side panels, wheel wells intruded into the express box, reducing the unobstructed width to slightly more than 48 inches. Express box length grew from 8 to 9 feet on the F-350. The width of the F-250 and F-350 stake bodies measured 82 inches. As with Ford's other light-duty trucks, the F-250 and F-350 were also available in cab only (for aftermarket bodies) or chassis-cowl form for special adaptations.

F-100 Panel Truck

The F-100 series also included a panel truck in the model line-up. This hauler, which has become a favorite of street rodders and truck collectors alike, offered an enclosed load length of 11 1/2 feet, when the passenger seat wasn't installed, or an 8-foot load capacity with both seats in place. A combination of a relatively low floor and high body provided an inside cargo height of 53 inches. Dual rear doors gave unrestricted access to the truck's interior for easy loading and unloading. The cargo-area floor was covered with plywood topped by metal skid strips.

Two panel delivery models (designated Type 82) were offered: a Standard and Deluxe. Although additional brightwork set the Deluxe apart externally, the most noticeable custom features were seen inside. Along with color-keyed, two-tone upholstery and harmonizing door trim, the Deluxe panel truck featured Masonite lining on the sides of the cargo area, full-length roof paneling, a foam-padded driver's seat, sound-deadener in the floor and above the headliner, armrests, a dome light, dual sun visors, bright trim on the instrument panel and window ledges, matching door locks, twin horns, a dispatch box lock, and an illuminated cigar lighter.

Despite the enhanced appearance and convenience offerings, in 1953 when you entered a truck, be it pickup or panel, it exuded masculinity. In a car the storage tray was called a glovebox, but on a truck it was a dispatch box. The Deluxe model featured a cigar lighter. The same item on a car was called a cigarette lighter. No doubt many truck operators used their cigar lighters for cigarettes, but the sales literature of the day wanted potential buyers to know that if they bought a Deluxe model, they'd have no trouble firing up their stogies.

Special Features

Nearly all the special features found on the Deluxe panel delivery were also available on the pickup—the omitted items being those like the Masonite cargo-area lining that applied only to the panel. Although many of the Deluxe features were simply dress-up items, the sound deadening was of practical value, as was the added seat padding, and locks on both doors. It had been considered common practice for years to equip trucks with just one door lock, on the passenger side. Apparently the engineer's perception was that truck drivers always exited on the curb side. This was a strange point of view since the practice never applied to cars, and for farm families in particular, a pickup was often the second car.

The twin-horn feature, too, was characteristic of a time when horns weren't used to blast your way through traffic, but for tooting hello to friends. Horn connoisseurs say that with one horn all you get is noise. Two horns are needed for melody.

Other extras included a rear bumper (standard equipment on the panel), tinted glass, a heater and a defroster, heavy-duty springs, and 6.00x16 six-ply or oversize tires.

For their golden anniversary trucks, Ford designers focused on styling and comfort as well as the traditional concerns of load capacity and pulling power. In driver

amenities the F-100 was several steps ahead of the competition. Chevrolet would wait until 1954 to offer a color-coordinated interior and automatic transmission, two of the new Ford extra-cost features. With the introduction of the F-100, Ford was making a statement that a truck doesn't have to be utilitarian only.

1953 Courier Sedan Delivery

For 1953 the Courier, now in its second season, received the annual facelift. The grille cavity was widened with the center bar extending around the front fender corners. The round parking lamps were replaced by rectangular ones and positioned in the grille cavity's lower corners. The round taillamps had an outer chrome ring and the same for the raised center reflector.

Besides the Courier nameplates and V-8 insignia (on vehicles so-optioned), the only external trim was a small brightmetal stone-shield on the quarter-panel bulge and a full beltline molding. The lower right corner of the rear door carried an *Overdrive* or *Fordomatic* nameplate when so-equipped. This one-piece door hinged on the left and

In the panel truck the passenger seat was an option because many of the businesses had no use for it. A plywood floor was standard with steel skid strips. The floor space measured 92.85 inches long (to the back of the driver's seat) and 62.25 inches wide.

opened wide. Glass area was generous, comprising one-third of the rear door. Such a clean design added to the appeal of Couriers for businesses concerned with their image.

Loading and unloading were done with ease as a door catch held the large rear door fully open. The fully lined and insulated cargo area provided maximum load space of 102 cubic feet. The floor length to the rear of the driver's seat measured 79 inches. In addition to the rear interior dimensions, there was a generous area for cargo next to the driver's seat.

Various wheel and tire combinations were available and relative to load capacities. They included: 6.70x15 four-ply tires on 5-inch rims, standard for a 4,000-pound GVW; 7.10x15 four-ply tires on 5-inch rims, optional for a 4,200-pound GVW; and 7.10x15 six-ply, optional for a 4,500-pound GVW.

The Courier's all-welded steel body was virtually dust-free and quiet. Headlining was a two-tone gray vinyl with the side panels of gray Masonite. Door panels were two-tone gray pressed board. The seat cushion and seat back were upholstered in brown wolf-grain vinyl.

The Courier's Flight-Style instrument panel featured a raised dome above the steering column, which housed the rainbow-shaped speedometer and gauges. The bezels illuminated on the combination starter-ignition switch and on the control knobs for wipers, headlights, vents, interior lights, and choke. The main instrument cluster had indirect illumination for the oil-pressure gauge, fuel level, water-temperature and battery-charge indicator, as well as the odometer and speedometer. The parking brake was operated by a T-handle on the lower left of the panel. A full line of passenger car accessories was available.

Colors for the 1953 Courier were Raven Black, Sandpiper Tan, Sheridan Blue, Timberline Green, Fern Mist Green, Woodsmoke Gray, Glacier Blue, Seafoam Green, Polynesian Bronze, and Carnival Red.

The new dashboards were sleek and clean looking, but had no radio grille. Radios were still a dealer-installed option. Interior door panels and the dash were always color-matched to the body.

The 1953 F-100 panel truck had a graceful design that has never been equaled in the truck field. The fenders and hood melded together to form a pleasing look that the public never got tired of seeing.

1953 Ford Truck Line-up

Ford advertised 21 truck designations and 194 models for 1953. They included 10 conventional F-Series models ranging from the Courier Sedan Delivery to F-100, F-250, F-350, F-500, F-600, F-700, F-750, F-800, and F-900 trucks. There were four Cab Forward (cab-over-engine) C-Series models: C-500, C-600, C-750, and C-800. There were four School Bus B-Series models: B-500, B-600, B-700, and B-750; and three Parcel Delivery P-Series models: P-350, P-500, and P-600. The new F-900 Series trucks were Ford's biggest truck models in history, with a maximum GVW rating of 27,000 pounds and a maximum gross cargo weight (GCW) rating of 55,000 pounds. Three 1953 models (F-100, F-250, and F-350) took the place of four

1952 models (F-1, F-2, F-3, and F-4). Two additional cab-over-engine models, the C-750 and C-800 Big Jobs, joined the former F-500 and F-600 medium-duty COEs.

It wasn't a forgone conclusion that the new model series would ever see the light of day. Product Planning Manager Chase Morsey recalls: "We had to go in front of the executive committee and fight to get the money to tool the new line of trucks because finance didn't want to do it. They didn't think we were making any money in the truck business. So we had to do a big presentation with all the facts. We finally got the new 1953 truck line approved, but it wasn't easy. It was a fight all the way." But Morsey also points out that all the areas from finance to engineering respected each other, and it was good business to question decisions.

Retail Prices

Retail price of a 1953 Ford F-100 6 pickup
$1,330.00
D & H (and Fed. tax or E.O.H.)
$100.30
Freight and transportation
$20.00
Factory-installed accessories:
gas, oil, and antifreeze, (5)
610x16 four-ply tires, heater
and defroster, oil filter,
wipers, and rear bumper
$69.53
Total delivered price
$1,591.22

Retail price of a 1953 Ford F-600 6 stake truck
$1,865.00
D & H (and Fed. tax or E. O. H.)
$158.30
Freight and transportation
$20.00
Factory-installed accessories:
Deluxe trim, (6) 750x20 eight-ply
tires, heavy-duty clutch,
aux. springs, oil filter, heater
and defroster, gas and oil
$302.40
Dealer-installed accessories:
Vac. brake booster
$41.31
Total delivered price
$2,516.65

Engines

The only component of the 1953 Ford trucks which did not change from 1952 was the engines. Engines for the F-100 through F-600 Series trucks consisted of the 101-horsepower, 215-ci, OHV Cost Clipper Six; the 112-horsepower, 254-ci, L-head Big Six; and the 106-horsepower, 239-ci, L-head Truck V-8. The F-700 used the 254-ci, L-head six. The F-750 Series used the 145-horsepower, 279-ci, OHV V-8 engine only. Ford's two biggest trucks, the F-800 and F-900 Series, used the 155-horsepower, 317-ci, OHV V-8.

F-100 Pickup

The 1953 model F-100 pickup had a curvaceous body style, including a wrap-around windshield and a large back window. Two new transmissions, Fordomatic or overdrive manual, became available so the driver could skip the gear grinding and double clutching, cruise easily on the highway with an overdrive gear, or skip shifting altogether with the first automatic in a Ford truck.

Norfolk plant worker George Bess remembers one day when one of the old-timers was under the hood of a new F-100 coming off the end of the line. Apparently the man would start each truck to test the engine. In this case, he didn't know the new automatic version was in reverse. Bess describes seeing him, after starting the truck, yelling and running after the truck as it idled across the plant floor. "Whoa, whoa!" he yelled as it hit the wall, fortunately doing little damage.

"Confidential"

In one information book marked "Confidential Advance Information on 1953 Ford Trucks" dated August 7, 1952, Ford International Engineering described the new models to marketing and sales. "The same engine assemblies that were used in 1952 were used in the 1953 trucks. As a result, only minor changes are contemplated in the cooling and exhaust systems so as to accommodate the new chassis. Some of the trucks employ the 1952 brake systems, but almost all the remaining chassis items are new. Also, almost all the trucks have new wheelbases.

"The 1953 trucks will be equipped with completely new appearing cabs. The cabs are greater in width, furnishing more hip room, and have a great deal more glass area. Among the features of the new cabs are a curved one-piece windshield, push-button door handles, a wider rear window (extending almost the entire cab width), an all-new lower and wider hood (blending into the fenders and providing better visibility), medallion on the front of the hood, and a new grille. The heater intake is on the right side of the cab; a cowl ventilator is still provided."

In fact, the memo wasn't completely correct. The six-cylinder engine for the all-new 1953 models was a 215-ci overhead-valve engine, the same engine as used in 1952. It produced more horsepower at a higher rpm.

In researching much of this information in the Detroit Library's National Automotive History Collection, most of the engineering blue-print sets of the F-Series were donated by Ford Motor Company. However, one rather detailed set had a stamp on the folder cover which read, "Please return to Chevrolet Division Library." Competition was stiff between Ford, Chevy, and International during those days, and much like today, all the big manufacturers bought, tested and tore down the competition's vehicles.

Another memo from a Ford budget supervisor said, "Please accept this memorandum as your authority to purchase the following vehicles," indicating prices and specifications for comparable model Ford, Chevy, and International 1 1/2 ton stake trucks, and directions on how to pay for them. "These vehicles will be used for experimental purposes and the charges should be applied to Engineering Development Order #31431."

F-100 Series Body Specifications
Pickup

The 6 1/2-foot pickup body continued to be of bolted steel construction with smooth side panels and no wheel-house obstructions. Box-type corner posts of husky steel were welded to the body. The box floor was of sturdy, seasoned wood protected by steel skid strips. Load space was 78 inches long, 49 inches wide, and 20.26 inches to the top of the flares; it yielded a 45 cubic foot capacity. There were four stake pockets in the corner posts for mounting uprights. The heavy, stamped-steel tailgate featured an overlapping clamp-tight panel design with a heavy reinforced edge. A new toggle-type latch clamped the tailgate firmly to body sides for a better seal. An anti-rattle drop chain held the tailgate firmly when lowered.

The passenger-side exterior mirror and spotlights were popular options in the 1950s. Ford offered several body colors in 1953 including Raven Black, Sheridan Blue, Glacier Blue, Light Green, Vermilion, Meadow Green, and Dovetone Gray.

Eight-foot panel

The panel's body was built from reinforced welded steel on the top and side panels with shaped and welded rear fenders. The driver's compartment was spacious, featuring a curved one-piece windshield with weather-sealed windows and doors. An individual-type driver's seat had 4 inches of adjustment fore and aft. A Deluxe version of the panel had many additional features for added riding ease, style, and driver efficiency. The panel's cargo-area floor was solid plywood. Steel skid strips protected the wood for long life. The floor was dust- and moisture-sealed at the side panels.

In the panel's interior, steel panels protected both sides from the floor to the top of wheelhouses. The panel had metal slats above the wheelhouses. The Deluxe panel had heavy Masonite lining above the wheelhouses on the panel sides. It also had a perforated headlining backed by

The F-250 stake-bed was a base model, shipped without hubcaps and no chrome teeth in the grille. It also had black trim around the windshield and wing vents.

These were Ford truck billboard signs planned for April and May 1953. They promoted economy in the heavy trucks and the all-new Fordomatic transmission in the F-1 series.

a thick glass-wool insulating pad extending the full length of the roof panel. The panel's load space was 92.85 inches long on the floor (138.5 inches alongside driver), 62.25 inches wide, and 53.20 inches high. Total load capacity (including space beside driver) was 155.8 cubic feet.

The panel's rear doors were hinged to a welded one-piece steel door frame and fitted with soft rubber seals. A two-position door check held the doors at 90 degrees or fully opened. The rear door opening was a generous 50.8 inches wide by 45.44 inches high.

1953 Production

In 1953, Ford took its biggest share (26.35%) of the truck market since 1938. Even though the start-up of an all-new truck was slow going, by March Ford production was in high gear and setting records. Then in April and May, production was hindered by supplier strikes. But after the strikes were over, production lines ran full tilt to the end of the model year. The market for the new Ford light-duty models (1/2-ton), accounted for more than half of Ford's 1953 sales. The next higher class (3/4- and 1-ton), accounted for about 17 percent of Ford truck production.

Ford posted these impressive numbers in a year when total industry sales actually decreased by one percent. All Korean War government-production controls on truck manufacturing dissolved in February 1953. Ford led in light-truck sales by increasing 21 percent to 654,000 units in 1953. Medium-duty sales slipped 10 percent and heavy-duty sales stayed flat.

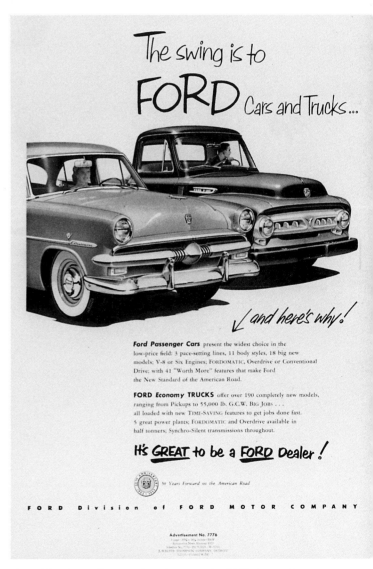

This ad for the Ford cars and trucks ran in the 1953 *Automotive News Almanac*. The J. Walter Thompson Advertising company handled all Ford Division advertising development and placement.

CHAPTER 7

1954 F-100 SERIES

L ife moved at a fast pace in America in 1954. Business was thriving and companies strived to keep up with the demands. Ford designed and engineered the new 1954 F-Series trucks to "get the job done fast!" This series was designed for the mid-1950s speed-hauling needs so companies could do their jobs quickly, efficiently, economically, and safely.

More than ever before, trucks had to meet higher performance standards. Because of the ever-increasing demands of modern business, trucks had to move goods swiftly. Trucks had to maneuver in and out of congested areas with ease and safety as well as keep pace with swifter-flowing traffic on mostly two-lane highways. Trucks had to be tough and dependable to stay on the job day after day and month after month. Time was becoming the biggest challenge to the truck-operating economy!

Ford engineers designed and built the F-Series trucks to meet and exceed the expectations of truck owners. The F-Series trucks did their jobs faster, handled more deliveries per hour, and made more trips per day. Drivers said they were the sweetest-handling trucks ever built. New Ford Driverized cabs reduced driving fatigue, which enabled drivers to accomplish more with greater ease, safety and efficiency. The new 1954 Ford F-100 pickup was, more than ever, America's No. 1 economy truck value. These trucks hauled big loads and saved money every mile. Owners could count on a long life of economical and reliable performance.

The 1954 F-Series had a huge, rather unsightly grille that led it to be one of the least collected F-Series models. The grille didn't have the same gracefulness as the previous model and included large "sergeant" stripes on either side of the V-8 emblem. The biggest news in 1954 was the demise of the flathead V-8 and introduction of the new overhead-valve Power King V-8s. The base model in the F-100 series produced 132 horsepower from 239 cubic inches. The old flathead was also a 239-ci engine.

221 New Models

The F-Series meant Ford's conventional line was made up of nine series—F-100 through F-900—with GVWs ranging from 4,000 pounds to 27,000 pounds, and GCW ratings of up to 55,000 pounds. There were 10 wheelbase lengths offered from 110 to 192 inches.

The 1954 Ford Triple Economy F-Series light-duty truck line introduced important savings into every fundamental phase of conventional truck operations. The hallmark of these trucks was economical operation: from the power plant, to the driver area, to the load-carrying capacity.

Think of Ford's Triple Economy concept as a three-legged stool. The first leg was "money-making power" from modern overhead-valve engines in both V-8 and six-cylinder configurations. Pistons in the 118-horsepower Cost Clipper six and the 132-horsepower Power King V-8 traveled a shorter distance per mile and at slower speeds, thus reducing friction and giving more usable hauling power. Ford truck engines were engineered to last longer and earn longer!

The second leg of the stool was "money-making convenience" due to Ford's new Driverized Cabs, available in Standard and Custom models. An array of driver conveniences such as excellent vision from larger glass areas in every direction, a three-man-wide seat with foam-rubber seat padding over non-snag springs, large wing vents and a cowl ventilator for fresh air combined to cut fatigue and conserve the driver's time and energy.

The third leg of the stool was "money-making capacities" from Ford truck's load-carrying ability designed to fit the owner's job. Ford engineers built strength into the truck's chassis and bodies, but kept their weight low. This translated into bigger payloads. Large payloads meant fewer trips and increased productivity and economy.

Total model offerings grew from 194 in 1953 to 221 in 1954. This growth came in the upper-medium and heavy-duty range. For the first time, Ford offered factory-built tandem axle trucks (T-700 and T-800 Series) and added the heavy-duty C-700 and C-900 cab-over-engine (Cab Forward) Series.

Body model offerings continued without change: The Courier, pickup, panel, stake, and platform F-100s; pickup, stake, and platform for F-250 and F-350s; and stake and platform only for F-500 and F-600s. All other series offered chassis and cowl or chassis and cab models only.

Ford F-100 Trucks

Although at a glance the 1953 to 1955 F-100s appear essentially alike, learning to recognize the different grille treatments is the easiest way to identify each one. For 1954 Ford stylists played on a variation of the 1951-52 frontal motif by attaching two angular supports to the horizontal grille bar, inboard of the headlights. In 1955 the grille would sport two parallel bars, as in 1953, but this time the upper bar would have a deep V-shaped notch in the center. The V intersected the lower bar.

The new F-100 6 1/2-foot pickup was the most versatile truck in the light-duty field. It earned a reputation as an economy leader due to its gas-saving six-cylinder engine producing more usable power at a low cost. Buyers could choose between the new 115-horsepower, 223-ci Cost Clipper Six and the new 130-horsepower OHV Power King V-8 engines. Both were guaranteed to get the job done. Because the tough cargo box contained 45 cubic feet of unobstructed load space, no hauling job was too tough for it. The all-bolted box construction delivered superior strength and longer life as it easily handled payloads of up to 1,500 pounds. The overlap design of the clamp-tight tailgate resulted in rigid construction and a grain-tight fit. Its seasoned wood floor was protected by steel skid strips for long life in heavy service.

Courier Sedan Delivery

The Courier for 1954 was styled along the beautiful lines of the new 1954 Ford automobile. Courier's impressive style provided prestige for businesses. The new grille featured round parking lights at each end of the main horizontal grille bar and a modern "spinner" located at the center of the grille bar. A new ball-joint front suspension improved Courier's ride, made steering easier, and lowered maintenance costs. Buyers could choose either the new 115-horsepower I-block Mileage Maker six or the new 130-horsepower Y-block V-8. Both engines offered high-compression performance with Ford's traditionally low fuel consumption. For driver convenience, buyers could choose the conventional three-speed transmission, a three-speed with overdrive, or the fully-automatic Fordomatic transmission.

The Courier offered safe protection for even fragile loads in its smooth interior. Maximum cargo protection was achieved by using 3/4-inch quality plywood for the floor and fiberboard on interior body sides. The headliner was padded with woven glass fiber. Load space was 102-cubic-feet big. Rear doors were hinged to remain open in any position. The large door opening width was 46.5 inches at the floor for faster, easier loading. Maximum GVW rating was 4,600 pounds on the 115.5-inch wheelbase chassis.

The New Y-Block OHV

The big news for 1954 was the new Y-block overhead-valve V-8 for the F-Series trucks. Called the Power King, this was a downsized version of the OHV V-8 that had been used in Lincoln cars and Ford heavy-duty trucks since 1952. The new engine had a displacement of 239 cubic inches and developed 130 horsepower at 4,200 rpm with a maximum torque of 214 foot-pounds.

This was more than merely a new engine, it was a complete-family-of-four new V-8 engines. The base 239-ci V-8 was the standard engine for light-duty trucks only. Ford engineers designed three additional deep-block truck engines. They included the 256-ci, 138-horsepower, Power King V-8 with 226 foot-pounds of torque; the 279-ci, 152-horsepower Cargo King V-8 with 246 foot-pounds of torque; and the 317-ci, 170-horsepower Cargo King V-8 with 286 foot-pounds of torque.

Ford's advanced design V-8 engine block provided greater structural rigidity due to its deep skirt, integral crankcase, and wide-base flywheel housing. These features provided the stability to support the crankshaft solidly and maintained precise bearing alignment.

All Deep-Block design engines featured overhead valves for the most efficient use of fuel. They also had high compression ratios to wring every bit of power from every drop of gas. The short-stroke design provided higher efficiency and longer life by reducing piston travel and lowered piston speeds.

As developments over the next few years would show, plenty of growth and performance capability was designed into this new V-8 engine. In its introductory year the new engine sported a mild 7.2:1 compression ratio and was fitted with a two-barrel carburetor.

New 138-Horsepower V-8 Engine

The new 256-ci Power King V-8 was derived from the Mercury automobile. This overhead-valve powerplant put out 138 horsepower at 3,900 rpm and could deliver 226 foot-pounds of torque at 1,900-2,400 rpm. It was the standard engine in medium-duty models including the school bus chassis, T-700 tandem-axle model, and C-600 and C-700 cab-over-engine trucks. This engine took the place, more-or-less, of the former Big Six, which was dropped after the 1953 model year.

New Cost Clipper Six

Though overshadowed by the new Y-block V-8, the six-cylinder engine also saw a substantial redesign for 1954.

Its new 223-ci displacement was achieved by opening the bore to 3.62 inches, while the stroke remained the same at 3.60 inches. The 223-ci configuration resulted in a low-wear, over-square design. The compression ratio had been upped slightly from 7:1 to 7.2:1 with a consequent boost in horsepower from 101 at 3,500 rpm to 115 at 3,900 rpm. Maximum torque output was now at 193 foot-pounds.

Although the new V-8 widened the performance margin over the six, the V-8 also added almost $100 to the truck's price. In six-cylinder form, the F-100 was economical to operate and could be driven off a dealer's lot for less than $1,600. No question about it, this six-cylinder truck represented a substantial value.

More Changes

Other changes for 1954 were largely comfort amenities. Seat upholstery was now woven vinyl. It was an attempt to avoid the sticky feel inherent to plastic seat coverings in hot weather.

The Fordomatic transmission was now available in the F-250 and single-wheel F-350, as well as the F-100 and Courier sedan delivery.

New options included a side-mounted spare for the pickup and express-bed models. Four-leaf auxiliary rear springs and power brakes were offered as an option on the F-100. Vermilion and Goldenrod Yellow were added to the color selections.

Ford's Driverized Cab

"Driverized" meant that Ford engineers and designers created a cab interior with the driver in mind. Their belief was that a comfortable and satisfied truck driver was more efficient and more productive.

Ford pioneered Level Action cab suspension. It "cradled" the cab in rubber-insulated comfort, dampened road shock, and resisted frame weave.

This rare Mercury version was produced in Oakville, Canada. Mercury's equivalent to the F-100 was the M-47. The "M" stood for Mercury and "47" stood for 4,700 pounds, the gross vehicle weight with the last two digits dropped off. *Ford of Canada Archives*

Driver comfort and convenience were definitely key. A "yard-wide" door opening let even the biggest driver swing in and out with ease. A big one-piece curved windshield, with swept-back pillars, allowed unlimited visibility. A large cockpit instrument cluster provided better visibility. Scientifically grouped controls for convenience and safety were easy to reach and easy to operate.

Ford provided all of the above comforts in the Standard cab. A Deluxe cab included all of these features plus 16 extras at a small additional charge. Ford was known to have the most luxurious cab in trucks.

The Year in Review

An economic slow-down in 1954 tightened market conditions and caused the return to competitive selling. The so-called "independent" truck manufacturers found themselves being squeezed tighter with each succeeding year. In 1948, independents accounted for 30.2 percent of total truck production. By 1954, their share had dropped to 21.8 percent. The Big Four—Ford, Chevrolet, Dodge, and GMC—grew stronger, while the independents—mainly International and Studebaker—slipped out of the competition.

The year 1954 was marked by a hotly contested battle between Ford and Chevrolet for the coveted truck-production title. Chevrolet won, but Ford managed to close the gap by a significant measure. Without a doubt, this battle of the titans determined the market share of the remaining truck industry producers.

Total truck production slipped 15 percent from 1953, but Ford's total production was only off by 5 percent. Most of Ford's decline was in light-duty models, as their medium- and heavy-duties sold well. Ford's share of the United States truck market reached 29.2 percent in 1954, its biggest share in history.

1955 F-100 SERIES

Chevrolet chose 1955 as the year to introduce its completely redesigned and re-engineered Task Force trucks. Ford trucks continued largely unchanged past the middle of the decade, as this was the third year for Ford's very successful F-100 Series. The Deluxe models were renamed Custom and several new dress-up features were added. Features included Custom nameplates on the doors, a brightmetal drip rail, a chrome upper grille bar, and stainless steel vent-window frames. One of the more useful new options was availability of two-stage rear springs for the F-100, which boosted the truck's GVW to 5,000 pounds.

Tubeless tires were adopted by the automotive industry in 1955 and they replaced tube-type tires on the F-100 that year, though the tire size remained 6.00x16. As is sometimes the case, not all improvements were for the better. The instrument pod now carried warning lights in place of the oil-pressure gauge and ammeter.

More Changes

New colors for 1955 fell in the cool range, with three new blues and a soft green. The Custom cab could be ordered in a two-tone combination of any body color plus a white roof and upper back-panel. The grille bars and wheels were painted off-white. The wheels formerly were painted to match the body color.

On the F-250 series, power brakes had become an option. The Timken rear axle, traditionally used in heavier Ford trucks, was replaced by a Spicer Model 60. Load rat-

The 1955 models brought the grille styling back on track with a more pleasing look. The Ford truck badge continued and overdrive-equipped models were identified just under the emblem. Badging on the side of the hood was a new Ford script with the model number noted within a chrome circle.

ing on the F-350 was increased by 600 pounds to a 7,700 GVW on the single-wheel models. These trucks also offered the power brake option.

A record number of 373,897 Ford trucks (all models) were produced in calendar year 1955—besting the company's previous production high set in 1929.

F-100 Series Engines

One change included a slight horsepower boost from 130 to 132 on the Power King Y-block V-8 engine and from 116 to 118 horsepower on the Cost Clipper inline six. Ford engines of this period were cast with deep skirt extensions, which gave substantial main-bearing and crankshaft rigidity. As a result, when looking at a 1950s-vintage overhead-valve Ford V-8 block, the casting has a distinct Y appearance. Correspondingly, the six-cylinder block was also deeper than normal, hence the I-block tag.

Cost Clipper Six

Ford's 1955 Cost Clipper Six was a thoroughly modern engine. Modern features included overhead valves, a short stroke (3.62-inch bore and 3.60-inch stroke) and a deep-skirted block. The Cost Clipper Six's pistons traveled a shorter distance and at slower speeds, which resulted in less wear and less power-robbing friction. They excelled by delivering more usable power from every gallon of gas. Attaining 118 horsepower at 3,800 rpm was excellent for a relatively small cubic-inch displacement. Full-length water jackets surrounded the cylinders to minimize bore distortion and reduce wear. A full-flow oil filter and a high-capacity oil pump ensured positive lubrication for long life. Higher compression, wedge-shaped combustion chambers made more complete combustion possible, which burned fuel efficiently and produced the most power from less gas.

The Power King

The Power King V-8's power provided fast, smooth acceleration—a big safety factor. The modern overhead-valve V-8 displaced 239 cubic inches and produced 132-brake horsepower at 4,200 rpm. Maximum torque was a potent 215 foot-pounds at only 1,800-2,200 rpm.

Compression ratios for both engines was 7.5:1. Like its six-cylinder companion, the Power King V-8 featured a short-stroke and deep-block design with full-length water jackets for cooler running even at idle or low speeds. Also like the

This F-600 model tank truck was used by Phillips Petroleum Company to haul gasoline to rural filling stations near Lebanon, Missouri. These units were normally equipped with the 140-horsepower Power King V-8, a 256-ci engine producing 228 foot-pounds of torque at 2,000 rpm. *Phillips Petroleum Company*

equipped with a full-flow oil filter and a high-capacity oil pump for positive lubrication and long life.

F-100 Models

F-100 models were by far Ford's largest selling trucks, totaling 152,916 units in 1955. Courier Panel Deliveries were included with the F-100s, not as a separate class, because they were a 1/2-ton model. Ford built a total of 124,842 F-100 pickups.

The F-100 pickup was built on a 110-inch wheelbase chassis. This was even more valuable in 1955 because of its increased payload rating (1,718 pounds) due to new rear springs. Drivers loved the new F-100; it was comfortable and easy to drive. Power braking and Fordomatic automatic drive—available at a slight extra charge—attracted many buyers. Driverized cabs in either Standard or Custom trim had a large array of driving conveniences, the most ever offered in a truck cab.

Both standard engines, the 118-horsepower Cost Clipper Six and the 132-horsepower Power King V-8, featured a modern, short-stroke design. These engines operated at slower speeds, thus reducing friction while producing more usable hauling power.

Standard F-100 bodies included the 6 1/2-foot pickup; an 8-foot panel in either Standard or Deluxe trim; and 6 1/2-foot platform and stake bodies. The platform body only accounted for 69 units sold, making it the lowest-volume model. Stake bodies, on the other hand, sold 997 units. These two bodies were essentially the same. The stake was a platform with the addition of stake sides.

Gross vehicle weight ratings for F-100 chassis and cab units ranged from 4,000 pounds to 5,000 pounds, depending upon tire size. The tires ranged from 6.00-16 four-plys to 6.50-16 six-plys.

Eight-Foot Panel Body

The 8-foot panel's interior featured a solid plywood floor with steel skid strips and was dust and moisture sealed at its side panels. The Custom panel had heavy Masonite lining above the wheelhouses on the panel sides and perforated headlining backed by a thick glass-wool insulating pad extending the entire length of the roof panel. Maximum loadspace was 96.9 inches at the floor (138.5 inches alongside driver), 62.2 inches wide, and 53.2 inches high. Total load capacity, including the space beside driver, was 155.8 cubic feet. Rear doors opened 50.8 inches wide to accept the largest cargo items. An individual-type driver's seat was standard equipment. An auxiliary seat and tinted glass were extra-cost options. Ford sold 11,198 Standard panels and 1,076 Deluxe panels in 1955.

6 1/2-Foot Platform and Stake Bodies

The floor of the platform and stake bodies was constructed of sturdy, seasoned wood. As in the past, it was protected by steel skid strips. The platform was a bridge-type construction, using heavy-gauge steel framing riveted to cross-girders, with steel angle-brackets riveted to the girders. Corners were reinforced with steel gusset plates. The sturdy stake racks were removable and constructed of straight-grain wood. Side and end sections were of one-piece construction. Load space on the platform was 85.6 inches long by 71.3 inches wide. The stake load space was 80 inches long by 67 inches wide and 29.5 inches high.

F-900 Ford's "Big Job"

Ford built its F-900 Big Job trucks to handle heavy loads with the operating economy expected only from a much smaller truck. These trucks featured rugged power and stamina, a stronger front axle, a 21,000-pound-capacity rear axle or optional two-speed axle with 7.17:9.77 ratios.

Ford offered 10 F-900 models on five wheelbase lengths: 132, 144, 156, 175, and 192 inches. Additionally, two types of tire equipment were offered, with each type supporting a separate GVW rating. Six 10.00-20 12-ply rated tires gave a 23,500-pound GVW rating, while six 11.00-20 14-ply rated tires gave a 27,000-pound GVW rating. Consequently, five wheelbases times two GVW ratings equals 10 F-900 models.

The only engine offered with these trucks was the 170-horsepower Cargo King V-8. Its cubic-inch displacement was 317, from a 3.80-inch bore and 3.50-inch stroke. Maximum gross torque rating was 286 foot-pounds at 1,700-2,300 rpm. This was Ford's mightiest engine. Its overhead-valve, short-stroke design was the most modern in truck use in 1955. Short piston travel and slower piston speed combined with relatively small cubic-inch displacement and high compression to develop high sustained torque with less engine effort. Engine blocks had a deep-skirt crankcase giving higher structural rigidity for smooth, long-lived performance.

Ford offered a full line of optional equipment and accessories to support its F-900 line. The list included single- or two-speed rear axles, heavy-duty five-speed Synchro-Silent transmissions with direct- or overdrive, and tires up to 11.00-22 14-plys. Also offered was vacuum-power-operated hydraulic or full-air brakes, heavy-duty rear springs, cast wheels and a mechanical tachometer. Master-Guide power steering reduced steering effort as much as 75 percent.

Ford sold a total of 2,014 F-900 models in 1955. The largest-selling model at 687 units was the 144-inch wheelbase chassis cab. These numbers did not include the F-900 series tandems or COEs.

1955 Parcel Delivery Chassis

Parcel delivery chassis were not important models in terms of absolute sales figures; they totaled 4,877 units in 1955. However, parcel deliveries were a legitimate model offering even though this market segment was limited. Ford was far better off dealing with a small volume series than letting a potential Ford customer buy from a competitor through default.

Ford offered two Standard parcel delivery models; the P-350 rated for a GVW of 7,800 pounds and the P-500 rated for 14,000 pounds. A P-600 chassis rated for 16,000-pound GVW was available on a special-order basis only. It differed from the P-500 only in its tire sizes—8.25x20 10-ply duals, verses 7.50x20 eight-ply duals. Only 67 P-600s were built in 1955.

Ford built only a chassis with windshield front end for the P-series. The front end consisted of a cowl, windshield, front quarter windows with straight door pillars above integral front wheelhouses, the grille, front bumper, two windshield wipers, and an adjustable tilt-forward-type driver's seat with folding back. The instrument panel was in front of the steering column. A steel toe-board with safety tread was on the floor. A heavily insulated engine cover was hinged at the right. Only the Cost Clipper Six engine was offered. Transmission options included the heavy-duty three-speed manual, four-speed, Synchro-Silent manual, and the Fordomatic automatic for F-350s only. Finish was in prime except for the grille and parking lamp frames, which were in Snow White. Ford sold a total of 4,877 parcel delivery chassis of all models in 1955.

Transmissions

Ford offered the industry's largest choice of transmissions, including: the three-speed manual, the heavy-duty three-speed manual, the three-speed manual with overdrive, the four-speed manual, and Fordomatic. The fully automatic Fordomatic became more versatile for 1955 with the addition of a low-gear "step-down" feature for faster acceleration and more power at the start.

The gas-saving overdrive enabled the truck to travel 43 percent farther at the same engine speed. Ford claimed a gas savings of up to 15 percent. The three-speed Synchro-Silent transmission was standard with overdrive. Also available were a heavy-duty three-speed and a four-speed transmission.

F-250 3/4-Ton

Three-quarter-ton models were built on a 118-inch wheelbase chassis and carried either an 8-foot pickup or 7 1/2-foot stake or platform body. Maximum GVW was 6,900 pounds and maximum payload was 3,013 pounds.

Standard engine choices were the same as for F-100 models: the 118-horsepower Cost Clipper Six or 132-horsepower Power King V-8. Transmission options included the heavy-duty three-speed manual with steering-column shifter, the four-speed manual, and Fordomatic.

F-350 1-Ton

One-ton models rode on a 130-inch wheelbase chassis and carried either a 9-foot pickup cargo box or a 9-foot platform or stake body. Maximum GVW rating was 9,500 pounds and maximum payload rating was 3,847 pounds. Engine options included the 118-horsepower Cost Clipper Six and 132-horsepower Power King V-8. Transmission options included the heavy-duty three-speed manual with shift lever on the steering column, a four-speed manual, and Fordomatic.

F-100 Courier Sedan Delivery

Ford's smallest and lightest truck for 1955 was again the Courier, a very handsome hauler indeed. Its styling for 1955 was new because all Ford cars received fresh and attractive sheet metal. The Courier was longer, lower, and wider than the previous Couriers. Its wider, flatter hood demanded a wider grille with a concave patterned mesh. Its hooded headlights were positioned directly above spinner-styled parking lights. The Courier was given a new wraparound windshield one year ahead of the other trucks. The bigger wraparound windshield dramatically increased glass area for improved driver vision and safety.

The Courier's sculptured fender sides, simple yet elegant, lent an air of prestige to Ford's lightest delivery vehicle. Some saw a touch of the upscale Thunderbird in its side profile, which was void of side trim, from the hooded headlights to the slightly protruded taillights.

The standard engine for Courier was the 223-ci Cost Clipper Six, which had been given a boost in horsepower to 120. New for 1955 was the 272-ci, Y-block V-8 rated at 162 horsepower. A "street machine" available directly from the factory.

In the interior Couriers boasted a new automobile-type instrument panel, with circular gauge pods and copper-tone coloring. The interior was upholstered in copper-tone vinyl.

Exterior colors included Raven Black, Banner Blue, Aquatone Blue, Waterfall Blue, Sea Sprite Green, Neptune Green, Snowshoe White, Pine Tree Green, Buckskin Brown, and Torch Red.

1955 Production

The truck industry turned in a good year in 1955, up 22 percent overall from 1954, but still far short of the record year set back in 1951 when slightly more than 1.4

million trucks were produced. Ford's total of 373,897 trucks showed an increase of 23 percent, or 1 percent better than the average.

The industry showed a shift toward heavier trucks and Ford also followed suit. In fact, Ford showed good increases across the board posting a very healthy 29-percent gain for F-100s and 24 percent for F-900s. Its lowest gain of only 5 percent was in the next to highest weight class (19,501 to 26,000 pounds). The demand for heavy-duty trucks came as a result of buyers feeling confident that Congress would pass the federal highway-building program. President Eisenhower did sign the act into law in 1956.

Ford's excellent showing in the over-26,000-pound category was surprising, because all other producers in this market sold more diesel-powered trucks than ever, and Ford only offered gas-powered trucks. Another development which was against Ford in this segment was the shift to tilt cabs, which Ford didn't offer in 1955. Still another significant developing trend in 1955 was a move to truck automatic transmissions. In 1955, automatics were confined mostly to light-duty trucks. Industry wide, 55,000 trucks were so equipped. There were 32,000 automatics installed in trucks in 1954.

Ford continued it's unrelenting pressure on arch rival Chevrolet for the coveted first place in sales. Ford managed to close the gap between them in market share by .4 percent. Ford rose to 30 percent, while Chevrolet fell .2 percent.

These F-700 Coke trucks had a gross vehicle rating of up to 19,500 pounds and came with 9.00-20 10-ply tires. A 140-horsepower, 256-ci Cargo King V-8 came as standard power. *Coca-Cola Company*

CHAPTER 9

1956 F-100 SERIES

The year 1956 was a great year in sales for Ford—car and truck manufacturing prospered. More than 1.8 million cars rolled out the plant's doors, and trucks reached an all-time high of 423,545.

In the Rouge Plant employee newspaper, the *Ford Rouge News*, the workers were given a sneak preview of the truck. "Company's 1956 Truck Line to Be Shown September 23," read the headline. The F-100 had many new additions to what was the basic 1953-56 body.

The last of this series of classic body styles was modernized with the wraparound windshield taken from the new Ford car. It improved forward and side vision compared to previous models, and the cabs were moving closer to the look and feel of the Ford cars. The 1956 models are considered by many to be the best looking Ford pickup ever built. Its stylish fenders, the new upper-cab design, and the car-like interior were conspicuous benefits. Another unique feature available on the 1956 was the full-wrap rear window. It was optional on all models and came with chrome moldings around all windows. The standard rear window was just over 4 feet wide and the cab had larger rear posts than the optional full-wrap version.

Other attractive styling features included headlights recessed into the grille. "Frenched" or hooded headlights had originated as a customizing fad, but by 1956 this headlight treatment could be found on nearly all domestic cars and most light trucks as well. A smart-looking, hooded instrument cluster, which closely resembled the Ford car layout, replaced the former gauge pod that Tom McCahill had described in his 1954 Ford F-100 road test as "untiring nice and plain." In addition, for the first time since 1938, a

Power steering and brakes were an option in 1956 along with Custom Cab interiors. The upgraded interiors included 5 inches of foam rubber in the seat base and 3 inches in the seat back. The seat covers were a combination of vinyl sides and woven-plastic top sides.

chrome-plated grille was standard on Custom Cabs.

The 1956 models had a new grille, dropping the 1955 V-center look. The new grille bars were straight across the front and clean looking. The V-8 models had the emblem in the center of the grille, but unlike the 1955s, there was no four-point star indicating a six-cylinder. There was no emblem or designation in the grille area if your truck was powered by a 223 Cost Cutter Six engine.

One of the more valuable improvements for these models was the change to a 12-volt system. This provided much better combustion at high rpm, far better starting power, and increased electrical accessories.

Ford boasted wide doors ("almost a yard wide!") in the three-man cab. The actual measurement was 33.6 inches wide. Ease of entry was the bragging point with the wide doors opening 70 degrees—wider than any other light truck on the market. The step-in height was easy in a Ford since they still used the low running board instead of the step-in inside the cab floor.

Some functional changes included a longer 8-foot pickup bed for the F-100 line and 15-inch wheels in place of the former 16-inch rims. Because the series was reaching the end of its run, rather than design a new frame to accommodate the longer box, the lighter trucks were simply fitted with frames from the F-250 models. Also for 1956, the gas tank, which had been relocated to outside the cab in 1953, was moved back inside.

Cab Comfort and Style

Seating in both the Custom and Standard cab models was a full three-across bench. The Standard cab used "shock snubbers" to absorb the bumps and keep the ride smooth. It had a combination of springs and padding with an adjustable seat back angle. The Custom cab was the luxury line for trucks with full foam padding. "Even the finest luxury cars offer nothing like this!" said the ads.

Dealer brochures were still done with illustrations, which made the vehicle look great. Everybody was smiling and the colors were brilliant. This ad shows the new F-100 with the "sun visor" roof. It's overhanging the windshield just enough to help shield the driver from the sun.

Both Standard and Custom model truck seats were fitted with a woven plastic upholstery that would allow air to pass through in hot weather. This kept the driver from sticking to the plastic on a warm day. The Custom cab also had either a red or a copper-tone vinyl bolster and facings to "harmonize" with the exterior finish.

The Custom cab had specific features beyond the Standard cab models, including the color-keyed upholstery, foam-rubber seat filling, door trim and hardware, headliner, sound deadener on the floor and rear cab panels, armrests on the left door, a dome light in the cab, twin sun visors, a cigar lighter, and fiber glass insulation on the forward cab wall. The now famous Magic Aire heater was still a part of the 1956 model option list.

The radio in the new models was a bit more advanced than previous models. The tuner and power unit were mounted on the left side of the instrument panel and the speaker and grille were on the windshield header. The antenna was mounted on the right cowl. One control knob

set took care of all adjustments. The center dial was for off-on and volume, the secondary dial was for tonal control, and the third outside dial was for station tuning. This dial could be pushed in for "rapid tuning." These radios also had the CONELRAD station settings, only to be used in case of "enemy attack or other emergency."

Safety and the Driverized Cab

Ford wanted the driver to "save with Driverized comfort!" The Driverized description had been used in Ford advertising for several years, but for 1956 the cab was really measuring up to creature comfort levels not attained before. For instance, the new wraparound windshield was now standard and it made the 1956 models stand out from all previous ones. It was billed as displacing 1,000 square inches and providing a commanding view of the road and traffic. "You gain a new feeling of confidence at the wheel that markedly relieves the strain of driving." This was part of the safety program Ford started with both cars and trucks in 1956.

Visibility Unlimited!

New full-wrap windshield . . . almost 1,000 square inches BIG, affords a commanding view of road and traffic. You gain a new feeling of confidence at the wheel that markedly relieves the strain of driving. Wide-set posts and deep side windows further add to "wide-open" visibility. Note smart windshield visor—a distinctive trademark of Ford's "Leadership Look" styling.

New full-wrap rear window gives Ford one of the largest all-around vision areas in any truck! Over 823 square inches in size, it's available for every cab and includes bright metal moldings around all windows. Even the standard rear window is more than 4 feet wide . . . up to 1½ feet wider than standard windows of other makes!

Real ease of entry!

Ford's roomy, 3-man cab is the easiest of all cabs to get in and out of!

Big doors, almost a yard wide, let the huskiest man step inside without a squeeze. What's more, doors open a full 70°, as much as 25° wider than other trucks! And there's ample room between the seat and the door post to swing your feet through.

For one of the most important driver-savers of all, check Ford's low step height. Instead of moving the running board up inside the door, Ford keeps it low . . . an easy intermediate step from ground to cab.

Roomy, deep-seated comfort!

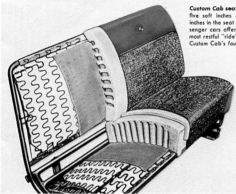

Custom Cab seat is full foam rubber— five soft inches deep in the seat, three inches in the seat back. Even the finest passenger cars offer nothing like this! It's the most restful "ride" in any truck! One of the Custom Cab's fourteen luxury features.

Standard Cab seat has exclusive shock snubbers that absorb jounce, smooth out the ride . . . plus non-sag springs and generous padding. Seat-back angle of both seats adjusts independently for most comfortable back support.

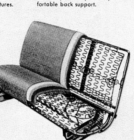

Free-breathing woven plastic upholstery stays cool in hot weather, won't stick to your body. Long-wearing and easy to clean, it's another feature Ford introduced to the truck field! Standard Cab upholstery is gray plaid pattern with red vinyl facings. Custom Cab has black and white chain-stripe upholstery with rich-looking vinyl bolster and facings. Bolster and facings are color-keyed, red or coppertone, to harmonize with exterior finish.

The dealer literature emphasized the comfort of the cab and the great visibility from the driver's seat. The seats were more car-like with heavy foam padding and there was ample room for three in the cab. Although seatbelts were an option, not many were sold.

The basic safety features Ford promoted in their trucks were Lifeguard steering wheels, double-grip door latches, and seat belts. The Lifeguard steering wheel was a deep-dish design. In case of an accident, the deep inset of the wheel would absorb some of the impact if the driver was thrown against it. The Lifeguard double door latches were exclusive in the market, giving extra protection against flying open during an accident.

Probably the most important addition, although the company may not have realized it at the time, was the seatbelt option. This was an industry first in any truck. The dealer brochure said that the belts, ". . . hold you securely in your seat . . . and greatly reduce the possibility of serious accident. They're available for both driver and helper at moderate extra cost." Oddly, although Ford initiated the safety campaign and installed seatbelts on its cars, this measure on behalf of the public had to wait for the consumer advocate movement of the 1960s, which charged the auto industry with being opposed to passenger safety, in order to capture public recognition.

For 1956, Ford trucks could be bought with power steering and power brakes. The Master-Guide power steering system cut driver efforts by as much as 75 percent. But like most power units during this period, the effort was so low that there wasn't much "road feel." The driver had to manually return the wheel to center since there wasn't much spin-back. The power brakes, whether hydraulic, air-hydraulic or air systems, were standard on F-600 models and up. At least one of the systems was available on all models.

Tires

Tubeless tires were standard equipment on all models, a truck industry first. For the F-100 models the 6.70x15-inch four-ply tires were standard, with a 7.10x15-inch six-ply optional. The tubeless tires could carry a bigger payload, and also ran cooler on the open road. A 16-inch wheel was also available with a 6.50x16-inch tire.

The F-100 came with a standard 110-inch wheelbase, but was also available in a 118-inch version as an 8-foot "express." This met the need for more carrying space—a total of 65.4 cubic feet. The regular pickup bed was 45 cubic feet.

Engine Options

"Short Stroke" was the engine theme of the day for 1956. Ford said the shorter the stroke, the less power-robbing friction, which would equal more efficient power. The standard engine was the 223-ci six-cylinder with 133 horsepower, billed as the most powerful and efficient in its class. The 223 Cost Cutter returned with improved breathing and higher compression.

With the advent of Chevrolet's hot V-8 in 1955, Ford and Chevrolet were now locked in a horsepower duel, a competition which gave spin-off benefits to truck buyers. With improved manifolding and higher compression, the standard Ford six developed 133 horsepower at 4,000 rpm. But the big news in the light-truck engine compartment was the addition of the 272-ci V-8, rated at 167 horsepower. The higher-output truck engines handled with ease the greater cargo capacity of the new 8-foot F-100 pickup boxes and the increased GVW ratings of 7,400 and 8,000 pounds for the F-250 and single-rear-wheel F-350 models respectively.

Enhancements to the V-8 engine came from improved cooling with better water circulation in the block, two chrome oil rings to reduce oil consumption, a crankshaft

Trucks with eight-cylinder engines had a "V-8" emblem in the center "V" portion of the grille. Those with a Cost Cutter Six had no grille emblem.

The new 1956 model F-Series trucks went on display in dealer showrooms on September 23, 1955. This was the first year that tubeless tires became standard equipment and eight exterior colors were available. One of the choices, Colonial White, was used as a second color in two-tone paint schemes.

vibration damper, longer-lasting 18 mm spark plugs, a fuel filter, and pistons top-plated with chrome for extended wear.

The optional 272 Power King V-8 engine (Ford persisted in calling it the "Y8" because of the engine block design) provided a snappy 167 horsepower. It was available in the F-100 through the F-700 models. When you considered the power-to-weight ratio, it was a virtual hot rod. The Power King engine series also came in a heavy-duty version with 158 horsepower and a lower torque range— 247 foot-pounds at 2,000-2,800 rpm.

Cargo King V-8 engines came in either 175-horsepower or Cargo King Extra 186-horsepower versions in the F-750 model. These models commonly were used for such jobs as beverage or petroleum delivery.

Ford claimed the new Torque King 332-ci V-8 series to be the mightiest engine in Ford truck history. The engine came in the Big Job models and produced 190 horsepower in the C-800 and C-900 series, with an optional four-barrel 200 horsepower

model available. The Torque King was based on the Lincoln V-8 engine. There was also a 302-ci version available with 175 horsepower and 279 foot-pounds of torque at 2,000-2,600 rpm. It was offered in C-750, B-750, F-750, and T-700 models.

Transmissions were still the Synchro-Silent style, with synchronized high-gears. The four-speed transmission was standard on Series F-, C- and B-500 through 700. A new five-speed medium-duty transmission was standard on the F-750 models and optional on the F-700. Three-speed transmissions were still standard on lighter models.

Overdrive in an F-100 was an "automatic" highway gear allowing the driver to cruise at a lower rpm on the open road. There was an overdrive control handle located under the instrument panel. When the handle was pushed in, the overdrive would automatically effect at any speed above 27 miles per hour in third gear, after easing up on the throttle. If the driver brought the truck to a speed below 21 miles per hour, the overdrive disengaged. If you pressed hard on the

F-Series trucks equipped with an automatic transmission had the Fordomatic identification just below the Ford truck crest.

The F-Series was available in either a 110- or a 118-inch wheelbase. The standard 223-ci six had 133 horsepower, but the 272-ci Y-block V-8 was rated at 167 horsepower—a virtual hot rod!

accelerator in high gear, the transmission would automatically drop back to third gear for more power.

The Fordomatic automatic transmissions had five positions on the selector: Dr (drive), N (neutral), Lo (low gear), R (reverse) and P (park).

F-100 Panel Delivery

The panel delivery continued as an F-100 with anachronistic styling that blended the trendy wrap-around windshield with outdated running boards and prominent fenders. Both the panel and pickup came in Standard and Custom trim packages. For 1956 new Custom features included a chrome grille, brightmetal windshield molding, and dash and inner door trim. Plated vent-window frames were no longer offered. The Custom upholstery weave was

now a black and white chain-stripe with red- or copper-toned facing. New exterior colors included Diamond Blue, Nocturn Blue, Meadowmist Green, and Platinum Gray.

F-100 Courier Sedan Delivery

The Courier was America's most distinctive Sedan Delivery in 1956. And it was also the most efficient. The Courier delivered the smoothest ride and easiest handling of any delivery vehicle. It had a Lifeguard deep-dish steering wheel and Lifeguard interlocking side-door latches for greater driving safety. Full-width seating for family use as a double-duty vehicle was available at extra cost. Standard was a single driver's seat. To make the driver's job even easier and more efficient, Fordomatic automatic was an extra cost option.

Continued on page 103

LOOK IN THE CAB!

Save with <u>Driverized</u> COMFORT!

Here's THE cab scientifically designed <u>around the driver</u> to make every driving operation simpler and easier. Its car-like comfort cuts fatigue, helps you get more done with less effort. It gives you new Lifeguard protection. And <u>only Ford</u> has it!

COLORS

Your choice of Vermilion, Diamond Blue, Nocturne Blue, Meadowmist Green, Platinum Gray, Goldenrod Yellow, Meadow Green and Raven Black. Attractive two-tone combinations—Colonial White on roof and upper back panel, plus any of above colors—are available on *Custom* Cab.

Whatever you want in a truck cab, you'll find it in fuller measure in Ford's '56 *Driverized* Cab *than in any other cab built today.* Car-like comfort for more relaxed driving . . . unmatched ease of entry . . . top all-around visibility . . . convenient, easy-to-use driving controls . . . new "Leadership Look" styling—*they're all yours.* Plus the extra protection that only Ford's exclusive new Lifeguard features are designed to give you!

Custom Cab with color-keyed red trim combination.

Exclusive new Lifeguard design!

Lifeguard Steering Wheel brings new security to truck driving. Exclusive deep-center design gives added protection against contact with the steering column in case of accident. With this and other new protective features, Ford answers a very real need of today's driver—and again points the way for the entire truck industry!

New Lifeguard Door Latches have exclusive *double* grip. They're designed to provide extra protection against doors springing open in an accident.

New Lifeguard Seat Belts help hold you securely in your seat . . . and greatly reduce the possibility of serious injury in an accident. They're available for both driver and helper at moderate extra cost.

6

An article in the Ford company paper, the *Rouge News*, outlined the features of the interior including the new deep-dish safety steering wheel. Ford said it would collapse, doing less damage to the driver in an accident. Seatbelts were also an option, and double grip Lifeguard door latches were standard.

The wraparound windshield was joined by an optional full-wrap rear window. The rear window option also came with chrome moldings around the rear window, side windows, and the windshield. The full-wrap option was available on any of the F-Series line-up.

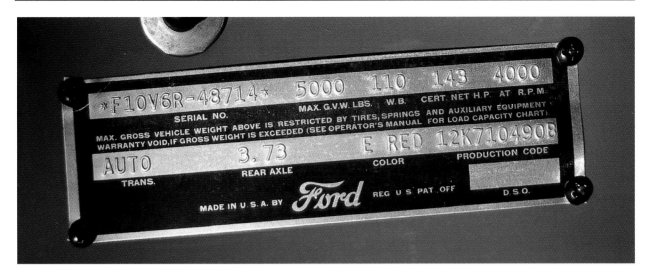

The rating plates listed quite a bit of information about the trucks. For instance, the first set of digits on this truck are F10V6R-48714. The "F10" identifies an F-100; the "V" signifies a 239-ci V-8; the "6" for 1956; and the "R" identifies the Richmond, California, assembly plant. The last series of numbers is the production sequence at that particular plant. A truck built at another plant could have the same serial number, but with a different letter to designate the plant.

The gauge layout had a half-circle speedometer that went from zero to 90 miles per hour and individual gauges for (left to right) the water temperature, oil pressure, odometer, battery charge, and fuel. These were very basic and the battery and oil were no more than "idiot lights." A long-neck mirror was optional for those needing better vision when pulling trailers or carrying bulky loads.

The F-750, considered one of the Big Job models when equipped with a 4V engine, had a hood scoop for providing extra air to the Cargo King Y-8s. The company called these V-8 designs "Y-8" because of the block design. They came in two versions: a 175-horsepower Cargo King and a 185-horsepower Cargo King Extra.

The pickup bodies came in two lengths: a 45-cubic-foot, 6 1/2-foot bed and a 65.4-cubic-foot, 8-foot bed.

Continued from page 99

The Courier had a fresh new grille for 1956. Its opening remained the same as in 1955 and was bordered with a bright wide band. New oval parking light pods located at the far ends of the grille added a distinctive note. A vertical center bar divider separated the concave, which had a pattern of five vertical bars on each side of the divider, crossing five horizontal bars to form large rectangular openings. Ford made front and rear bumper guards standard equipment for 1956. An engine identification badge, an I-block six or Y-block V-8, was located on the lower front of each front fender.

The side-hinged, single, rear door was 46.9 inches wide at the floor, and was 32.1 inches high. The door would remain open at any position for ease of loading and unloading in tight quarters. The full-interior vinyl lining looked smart and protected the load. Door panels were smooth-pressed wood in the same medium-brown color of the side panels. Cargo area was 6 1/2 feet long and over 5 feet wide—102 cubic feet of load space in all, plus space beside the driver's seat.

The instrument panel was all new for 1956. All instruments were placed in a cluster under a shrouded visor, circular in shape. Dial faces were finished in black with white lettering making them easy to read.

Engine names and displacements were carried over from the previous year, but slight power increases were noted. The 223-ci Cost Cutter Six was rated for 133 horsepower versus 120 horsepower in 1955. The Power King V-8 was rated at 167 horsepower versus 162 horsepower in 1955.

Dealer Accessories

Dealer-installed accessories were becoming a much bigger business by 1956. These accessories were generally provided to the dealer by Ford and promoted in the Ford sales literature. Here is a sample list of 1956 options and a Ford description and part number:

- **Seat cover.** Ideal for truck use. Heavy-duty fiber in a colorful plaid pattern is long wearing. Part No. BAAA-18627-A

- **Splash Guards and Brackets.** Designed to meet state requirements and give lasting, efficient service. Heavy-gauge molded rubber Part Nos. 2C-16412-A (24"X24") 2C-16412-B (24"X30") 2C-16412-C (24"X36") 2C-18697-B (brackets)

- **See-Clear Windshield Washer.** "See-Clear" for easier, safer driving. When dust or traffic film blur your view, just press the foot plunger. Part Nos. TAAA-18293-A, CPA-19550-A (solvent)

- **Reflector Flare Kit.** Compact and convenient. Three red reflector flares, three red flags and steel flagstaffs in easy-to-store metal box. Part No. 8C-18286

- **Truck Road Lamps.** Wide, low beams make driving safer and easier in fog, rain, and snow. Big, sturdily mounted lamps can be easily adjusted as required. Part No. FAE-18207-A

- **Hand Brake Signal.** Helps avoid unnecessary brake wear. Red light flashes a warning if you start the truck without having first released the hand brake. Part No. FAD.18159-A

- **Fire Extinguisher.** Handy, dependable protection for truck and payload. Smothers gasoline, oil, paint, and electrical fires with vaporizing liquid. Bracket holds it securely yet permits quick removal. Part Nos. TAAA-18370-A, TAA-19547-A (Refill liquid)

- **Extension Arm Mirror.** Affords a clear view to the rear on maximum width bodies. Can be extended, raised or lowered as required. Six-inch reflecting surface. Part No. BAAA-18402-B

- **Mirror Arm Brace Kit.** Gives extra rigidity to extension arm mirrors—convenient when driving over rough roads. Part No. 2C-18337-A

- **Front Tow Hooks.** A big help in emergencies which require pulling or towing. Forged from high-quality steel, engineered to withstand great stress. Part No. TAAA-18245-A

- **Governors.** Save gas, oil, brakes, and maintenance with a Ford engine governor. Available for all six-cylinder O.H.V. and eight-cylinder "L" head engines. RPM ranges from 1,500-3,600. Part Nos. EAG-18204-A,B EAJ-18204-A, B8RC-18204-E,F

- **Stop Light.** Gives unmistakable warning of your intention to stop. Giant light flashes on the instant you apply brake pressure. Part No. FAA-13640-A

- **Locking Gas Tank Cap.** Guards against gasoline theft and tampering. Heavy-duty construction with high-quality tumbler lock and snap-down cover. Part No. 8A-18168 A

- **Engine Compartment Light.** Makes it easier to check and pour oil, or inspect engine in dim-lit surroundings. Switches on automatically when hood is raised—turns off when hood is lowered. Part No. FAC-18375-A

CHAPTER 10

MERCURY TRUCKS

The year after Henry Ford started producing vehicles in the United States, Ford Motor Company Canada started building Ford cars and trucks at their Windsor, Canada plant. The year was 1904. Located just across the Detroit River, it was the first international production venture for Ford.

The Windsor plant began producing the new F-Series in late 1947, about the same time as the U. S. plants, and had an on-sale date of January 23, 1948, only a week after the United States. Both Ford and Mercury models were produced to sell in the separate dealerships. Although identical underneath, they had minor trim changes to separate them in the market place. The Mercury trucks were billed as slightly upscale, as were the cars, and the base price was $37 higher than its Ford cousin. The Ford F-47 was $1,398 and the M-47 was $1,435.

Of course, the "M" stood for Mercury and the "F" for Ford. The model designation stood for the gross vehicle weight. The "47" was the 1/2-ton model with the last two zeros dropped off. An M155 would be a Mercury 15,500-GVW model. Model designators in 1951 and 1952 were M-1, M-2, and so on. This method of identifying the models continued until 1953, when Canada adapted the U.S. system such as F-1000, F-250 for Fords and M-100 and M-250 for the Mercurys. The Canadian plants also produced both right-hand-drive (RHD) and left-hand-drive (LHD) trucks.

On 1948–1950 trucks only, the model designations had some logic behind them. For instance, the "M" stood for Mercury and the "47" was derived from the gross vehicle weight with the last two digits removed. An M-47 would be a truck with a 4,700-pound GVW. *Ford of Canada Archives.*

The Big Debut

The Mercury name on a truck came into being for the first time in 1946 in Windsor. A March 20, 1946, press release form the Ford of Canada News Bureau stated, "Carrying the name 'Mercury' into the commercial hauling field for the first time, a new line of Mercury light and heavy trucks will be introduced across Canada this Saturday in showrooms of Mercury and Lincoln dealers."

From the home office in Windsor, the public relations department put out a release for news editors "submitted solely on a basis of news value" on January 20, 1948, to announce the all-new model Mercury trucks. "A newly designed cab in which the seat rises as it is moved forward to accommodate the driver of shorter stature is a feature of the new Mercury trucks for 1948." Behind the seat was the fuel tank, which used to be under the seat. A tool box was placed on top of the tank and the press release pointed out that "there is ample room for jack and flares at either end of the tank." Keeping your flares on top of 20 gallons of gasoline positioned behind your seat might not have been the best of ideas!

All Canadian trucks had only V-8 engines. The 223-ci six-cylinder wasn't available until 1957. Two flathead 239-ci V-8 engines were offered: one for light duty and "high-speed service," and the other, designated the Mercury 188, for heavy-duty hauling. These engines covered the whole range of trucking operations. One smaller engine developed maximum torque of 180 foot-pounds at 1,850 rpm and powered the two light-duty models. The bigger engine developed a maximum torque of 188 foot-pounds at 1,400 rpm to power the four bigger, medium-duty models. Both engines had aluminum cylinder-heads and aluminum-alloy pistons and cylinder-bore

The Windsor, Canada, Ford assembly plant began producing Mercury "M-Series" trucks only a few days after the U.S. plants started their production. Ford of Canada started selling Mercury trucks on March 20, 1946. The advertising tag line was "Smartest truck line ever built." *Ford of Canada Archives*

All Canadian Mercury trucks had V-8 engines. The M-180 V-8 was a re-badged 239-ci flathead. They had two-tone paint jobs unique to Canadian production. *Ford of Canada Archives*

Ford of Canada had their own advertising agency to develop the billboards and print ads. Ford produced and sold the full line-up of trucks from light to heavy. *Ford of Canada Archives*

The 1954 M-Series was still the same as the U.S.-built Ford trucks with Mercury badges. Collectors search out the Mercurys because of their low production volumes compared to their U.S. cousins. *Ford of Canada Archives*

This unique C-800 cab and car hauler was used by the Bill Stroppe racing team to carry their Lincolns to the Mexican Road Race in the 1953 event. Since Stroppe was sponsored by Lincoln, he figured it would be appropriate to drive a Mercury product. *Bill Stroppe & Son, Inc.*

life. They had modern-type valves and crankshafts to give linger life for more profitable trucking.

Cab Comfort

The cabs in these models, like all other F-Series pickups, used the Level Action suspension to insulate it against vibration, noise and "frame weave."

The 1948-50 cabs had increased visibility for the driver and passengers due to a one-piece windshield with a greater glass area than previous models. It also had no center post and was 2 inches higher "so that tall drivers may see forward without stooping." Ford also claimed that the angle of the windshield had been positioned to reduce glare, reflection, and driver fatigue. The corner pillars were also stronger.

The new models featured the three-way air-control system including adjustable window ventilator panes, and a cowl ventilator. The third part was the optional heater and fan.

The Line-up

Mercury truck line-up included a 1/2-ton pickup and panel with a 4,700-pound GVW rating; a 1-ton pickup with a 6,800-pound GVW rating; and a 1 1/2-ton stake with a GVW rating of 10,500 pounds. Also in the line-up was a 2-ton series on three wheelbase lengths, offering a GVW rating of 13,500 pounds; and a 3-ton series on three wheelbase lengths offering a GVW rating of 15,500 pounds. A 3-ton 194-inch school bus chassis was also available.

Ford of Canada's advertising theme was "It's the Smartest Truck Line Ever Built." It probably wasn't the most creative line an agency has ever come up with, but it seemed to get the job done. Canadian sales were only about 10 percent of the U.S. truck sales.

CHAPTER 11

F-100 FERVOR

In the 1950s those who bought new Ford F-100 pickups thought of their trucks as tools. They certainly did not see these vehicles as an object to be cherished, adored, and admired, the status to which these trucks have risen.

I distinctly remember the 1953 F-100 pickup my girlfriend's father bought new in 1953. He was a farmer and a "died-in-the-wool" Ford man. The F-100 was the first new vehicle he had ever bought. It did double-duty as his farm work truck and the family's personal transportation. He was mighty proud of his new Ford. Given any opportunity, he would gladly tell you it was the best pickup ever made. Talking about it was the extent of his love affair with his Ford pickup, however. He worked it hard and never hesitated to haul whatever needed moving. Nor did he garage his truck or ever wash it. Trucks in those days were not pampered; they worked.

America's love affair with pickups didn't begin until the 1960s and then took off in the 1970s and 1980s. Pickups in the 1950s were, for the most part, tools of the trade for the farmer, tradesman, construction worker, merchant, public servant, and others. It would not be fair if we didn't recognize that some buyers in the 1950s purchased their pickups for personal transportation, although it was a very small minority. As a matter of fact, it was at that time when the Big Three first began to make an effort to promote pickup sales for personal transportation. An obvious case in point is Chevrolet's 1955 Cameo Carrier—an upscale pickup with a dual mission in life if there ever was one. The Cameo prompted Ford to follow up with its car-based Ranchero pickup in 1957. Dodge quickly followed suit in 1957 with its unique Sweptside pickup. International's cab-wide, high-style Golden Jubilee Custom Pickup with a "Sweep-Around" windshield was first seen in March 1957.

But these early enticements for pickups as personal transportation didn't have a great deal of impact on men or women. Pickup sales didn't begin to seriously increase until pickups became more civilized. The rise in the popularity of pickups correlates to equipment such as automatic transmissions, various power assists, independent front suspensions, more comfortable seats upholstered with attractive color-keyed fabrics, and modern upscale styling.

F-100 Tops the Charts

No other truck, or car, at any time has caused such fervor. To the army of F-100 pickup aficionados, these trucks reached the status of "cult" vehicles in the mid 1960s. It begs the question, why have the F-100 pickups achieved this status while the F-1 Bonus Built pickups have not? The F-1s were great trucks too. No one would argue otherwise. They were well built, stylish, powerful, and all that, but they are not held in the same high esteem as the F-100s. There is probably no one right answer to this question, but I'd like to advance mine.

I think it's due to the F-100's outstanding styling and driveability. And not merely good styling, but phenomenally different and unique. The correct term is "Advanced Design." No other pickup in 1953 came close: not Chevrolet, not Dodge, not International, not Studebaker, not Willys, not anybody. In engineering terms, the F-100 didn't plow new ground, except for a couple of key chassis engineering changes. Its overhead-valve six-cylinder engine was a great new engine when introduced in 1952, but Chevrolet trucks had been powered by an OHV six-cylinder since 1929. Its fully automatic Fordomatic transmission was a first for a pickup and certainly important, but automatics had been around in cars for several years by 1953. The F-100's success proves that the most important consideration for anything bought is style, looks, or aesthetics. If a product doesn't look "good" to the customer,

1953 was a very good year. The chrome teeth are still in the grille, indicating that this was once a Custom cab, but little else is stock.

Many early F-Series trucks are turned into full-blown hot rods, but most are just modified into something beyond stock or original. This 1950 model F-1 has some basic modifications such as fender markers, cab-top lights, and trailer mirrors that weren't available during the early 1950s.

The most common modifications on the F-Series are paint and high-wear interior items such as seat covers and floor mats.

Two-tone paint wasn't an option on the F-Series until 1956. This 1949 model, although not too far from original appearance, has silver and pewter two-tone paint and add-on side boards.

whether it's a truck or a pair of shoes, it will be passed over in favor of a competing product, which has greater "eye" appeal.

Cab Styling

An analysis of what set the F-100 pickup apart from every other pickup of its day must begin with the styling of its cab. Cab styling is a function of clever design and sound engineering. The F-100 had "The cab designed with the driver in mind." Ford didn't use this term, but certainly could have. Their official term was "Driverized" cab. In the early 1950s all truck designers had the driver in mind. The point is, Ford designers did a better job! They designed a cab with much greater glass area, including a wider back window than ever before. Have you ever driven a pickup from the 1940s and early 1950s? Every one of them had a tiny back window. Rear vision in these

trucks was difficult to the point of being dangerous!

Other features of the Ford Driverized cab included a wider seat and 5 feet of hip room. The F-100's seat was well-built and comfortable, even for three men (the F-1's cab was only adequate for two). It was constructed with new non-sag springs and Ford's exclusive new Counter-Shock seat construction, which absorbed road shocks for a softer, smoother ride. For the first time the cab's interior was attractive with harmonized colors, new trim, and a handsome instrument panel with easy-to-read instruments and conveniently located controls.

The Chassis

Now let's look at the new chassis engineering features, which contributed to the F-100's driver appeal. First, a new set-back, wide-tread front axle yielded a shorter wheelbase and greater maneuverability. The front

This fire engine red paint wasn't the same as the Vermilion on the originals, but the truck is still used on a daily basis almost 50 years later.

This 1948 model F-1 panel was completely modified with a custom interior and a lowered, smoothed-over exterior. It was made to tow this 1934 Miller Indy car to antique car events.

This owner added custom wheels and tires along with a candy apple red paint job. The wing vent glass has been etched and custom side boards are mounted on the bed.

axle supported a larger share of the load for better weight distribution. The set-back front axle and wide-tread stance resulted in a shorter turning radius and easier handling. Turning diameters were shortened by up to 14 percent. The driver's ride was improved by these same new engineering features. With a shorter wheelbase, the driver was positioned nearer the easy-riding front springs. And, longer springs and shock absorbers gave a smoother ride.

Ford also boasted of other engineering improvements such as a stronger Hypoid rear axle, removable brake drums for easier maintenance, a non-whipping tubular drive shaft, and a new deep-channel frame. Unseen mechanical improvements are expected and necessary for a better operating truck. But be assured they don't mean much to a driver/owner compared to a roomy cab with a wide comfortable seat, a shorter turning diameter, better maneuverability, a softer ride, better vision in all directions and the passenger-car ease of steering-column shifting. In 1953 Ford engineers switched to all-synchronized three- and four-speed manual transmissions. If you have ever driven an F-1 Series truck with a "crash box," you'd love the F-100's new Synchro-Silent transmissions. These practical, real-life improvements made a deep and lasting impression on drivers in 1953 and on those who have driven a F-100 series truck since.

Spotlights were a dealer option, but the louvers and hot rod red paint weren't.

This 1948 F-1 is hardly recognizable with all the body work done to the bed. The tailgate is completely welded to the box.

The F-100's succulent style, roomy and comfortable Driverized cab, a Synchro-Silent manual transmission, and fun-to-drive new wide-tread set-back front axle made the F-100 a lethal driving machine. These trucks have also stood the test of time. These are the reasons for F-100 owner's cult-like devotion to their trucks.

Ford F-100 Mission

Let's make one thing perfectly clear. The formidable success of the F-100 trucks did not happen by luck or happenstance. No way. Beginning with the Bonus Built trucks in 1948, Ford's management was on a mission. Henry Ford II's objective, and that of his carefully selected management team, was to overtake Chevrolet and be No. 1 in car *and* truck sales. A quick check of the numbers shows that in every year from 1948 to 1956, Chevrolet continued to hang on to its truck production leadership position. Ford's management would have been delighted to overtake Chevrolet at this time, but they were realists enough to know their goal wouldn't be reached

quickly. They would, however, keep on trying until they succeeded. This wasn't a battle, this was war. Ford expected to win some and lose some in the short run, but in the long run they expected a total victory.

One step at a time may be the best way to describe Ford's long-term strategy. The Bonus Built series accomplished its purpose, which was to put Chevrolet on notice that Ford trucks were back. The F-100 series seconded that notice with greater emphasis.

The phenomenon of the marketplace is that when you are No. 2 you cannot afford to be only "just as good" as No. 1. You have to be better. So much better that buyers clearly recognize that fact. In order to succeed, No. 2 must make a product statement buyers won't miss. There you have Ford's 1953 to 1956 F-100 Series pickups. Not merely good, but excellent. As Dodge would say years later, "The rules have changed!" Chevrolet from that time forward would be forced to pay close attention to and examine every move Ford made. Imagine what would have happened to the truck market if the F-100 pickups

The 1948 model was clearly a good design to customize. This one is lowered, painted, and now has most of the comforts of a current-model pickup.

had been a bomb! Ford would have tried again, no doubt, but the wind would have been taken out of their sails. Chances are that Chevrolet maybe never would have relinquished its No. 1 sales position. Ford's management understood how critically important the F-1 and F-100 trucks were to their long-term goal of overtaking Chevrolet as the following quote from the F-1 Series truck's salesman's guide shows. "What is important is that the Bonus Built story, and all that goes with it, does a constructive job of building tomorrow's sales today in order to gain our objective of leadership in truck sales."

Hot Rod Collectors and Restorers

Because of their success, or because of what they are, the 1953 to 1956 F-100s have lived on. Ford built almost 530,000 F-100 pickups and panels. A big percentage of

that total has survived. A whole industry has emerged to serve F-100 owners with parts and accessories to aid in restoring F-100s to original condition or for street-rodding. As with many auto-related phenomenons, the street-rodding of F-100 trucks began in California and moved east.

Pickups and pickup lovers are everywhere. F-100 clubs have sprung up from coast to coast. In the early years some of the clubs met up to three times a month. Clubs tend to be social "melting pots" attracting members from all walks of life, and with many professions represented. Members help each other with their particular skills and or abilities.

Let's look at the reasons why collectors and street rodders choose their F-100. First, the 1953 is picked because it was the first pickup of the F-100 series, it was

Motor City Flatheads of Dundee, Michigan, builds flathead V-8s for people restoring original Fords as well as for those who want 300-horsepower hot rods. This flathead had a B&M blower and all the latest horsepower add-ons.

the last year for the famous Ford flathead V-8 engine, and it was Ford's milestone 50th anniversary truck. It's not very often that you find two opposite milestones in one vehicle. The first of a series and the last of a world-famous engine. The 1954 F-100 is of special interest because it is the first light truck with an overhead-valve V-8 engine, the 239-ci Power King.

Others prefer the 1955 model because of its new grille featuring a V-shaped upper grille bar. The choicest F-100s are the 1956 models, because they were the last of the series, but beyond that they are favored for their distinctive wraparound windshields and "big back windows." The 1956 Custom cab trucks are the ultimate because they have a chrome grille. A higher percentage of 1956 trucks were sold with the Custom cabs than in pre-

vious years, and they also have the more desirable 12-volt electrical systems.

Typically, we think of a restored or street-rodded F-100 Series Ford as a pickup—and most are. But in addition to pickups, the panel trucks are also highly sought after. There is a certain amount of utility a panel offers that a pickup can't, and vice versa. Other owners prefer the look of a platform body. Their mostly wooden bodies are attractive and easy for an owner to build as compared with an all-steel pickup cargo box.

Another F-Series truck type growing in popularity with restorers and street-rodders are the 1953 to 1956 F-500 and F-600 cab-over-engine trucks. These husky haulers can be crafted into the ideal flat-bed collector car or pickup hauler. Other restorers prefer a short wheelbase

This yellow F-100 is lowered, the cab is chopped, and the hood now tips open from the rear. The 1956 models are easier to find than most of the earlier F-Series and therefore more popular to restore and modify. The 1956 is considered one of the best-looking pickups of all time.

Wide tires and independent suspensions are a common modification. Notice the new gas filler door at the rear of the fender.

A Cleveland 351 Ford V-8 producing well over 300 horsepower fits snugly into a 1953 F-100. The engine is hooked up to an automatic transmission and the cab has air-conditioning, plush upholstery over custom seats, and a full stereo system.

COE as a tractor for pulling a trailer to carry one or two collector cars or light-trucks. These medium-duty COE trucks are usually not modified in the same manner as F-100 pickups. For the power needed to cruise the interstate, owners replace the original engine with a more powerful V-8, most often used in combination with an automatic transmission. Certain creature comforts are added such as air conditioning, modern seating, sound systems, and additional engine gauges, to name a few. Glitz and glamour items are not deemed to be significant for these modern versions of a historic work truck.

There is a movement now among the F-100 crowd for authentic restorations as opposed to street-rodding because these trucks are getting harder and harder to come by. Another growing trend is the move to heavy-duty models, F-600s to F-900s, for two reasons. First, is the scarcity of F-100s and second, there is a growing interest in the hobby with larger trucks in general.

Heavies were not built in the same quantities as lights, but still they are available. Prices are reasonable and parts are out there. Big rigs are "head-turners."

Street-rodders love all F-100 series trucks for the simple fact that they feature the maximum in "unbolt-ability" for ease of restoration. Fenders can be unbolted and removed for any needed body work. For that matter, the cab and pickup box can be unbolted for ease of restoration work too.

Beyond the ease of "unbolt-abilty" there is the additional advantage to these trucks of being able to adapt and interchange at the owner's preference. Owners can do just about anything that they can imagine—and most do. It seems to be a contradiction, but the appeal of these trucks is that many, if not most, owners turn them into "luxury passenger cars" with modern suspensions for a better ride and beautiful interiors and modern accessories for comfort and ease of handling.

This 1953 Ford is capable of faster 0-60 times than most super cars sold today.

Another advantage of rodding a truck is that its huge engine bay will accept any modern replacement engine an owner chooses—Ford's 351 Windsor or 390 V-8s, Chevy's rat motor, a huge Mopar Hemi, or any of several other GM built V-8s, small or big block versions. Any of these engines are an easy swap even with an automatic transmission hooked on back.

F-100 Customizing

The typical customizer will start his project by stripping down the truck to the bare frame and building it back up. While the truck is down to the bare essentials, the owner details the chassis and rebuilds by adding a passenger car front section with independent front-coil-spring suspension for more riding comfort. Most owners prefer either a Chevelle or a Volare front end. Other owners opt for a torsion-bar front setup from a 1950s-era Chrysler-built automobile. A front disc brake system is another popular change. And power steering too, of course. Regardless of the extent of modifications made to the frame, suspension, brakes, engine, transmission, and other changes which are not readily apparent to the naked eye, the basic body, cab, and fenders are left intact. Generous amounts of chrome and special paint schemes show even the casual observer that this is not a bone-stock truck.

A visual highlight of almost all F-100s is its beautiful, highly polished wood cargo box bed. Well-finished oak planks with gleaming chrome skid strips draw attention to the fact that this vehicle is a truck, and a truck is all about hauling stuff. Pay no attention to the fact that its hauling days are over, the mere fact that it was built to haul is what's important.

The truck's engine bay is its second most highly visual treat. The engine itself and the engine's plumbing and accessories are plated as much as possible with gleaming chrome accented by splashes of colorful wiring and braided hoses. The owner's goal is to let the gleam light up the bay. What you won't see are any traces of oil, dirt, dust, rust, or water spots. Its critical for the engine bay to be absolutely surgically clean, neat, and orderly. And the bottom line is that it is all very tastefully and professionally done.

Inside the cab are all the comforts of home in the typical F-100 streetrod. A deeply upholstered bench seat is common, while twin bucket seats are favored by others. Other comfort sources are an air conditioning unit and elaborate music systems featuring tape and CD players. Often a CB radio and modern seat belts replace the original primitive units. Owners generally supplement the truck's factory gauges or "idiot" lights (1956 trucks only) with more informative, generally Stewart-Warner, oil-pressure and amp gauges.

The interest and enthusiasm in the trucks built by Ford between 1948 and 1956 have enabled these trucks to live on.

Ford Motor Company designed this "50 Years" logo to celebrate a half-century anniversary of the F-Series in 1998.

APPENDIX

Appendix A: F-Series Factory Body Colors

1948
Barcelona Blue
Vermilion
Arabian Green
Chrome Yellow
Black
Birch Gray
(Meadow Green replaced Arabian Green in the
   Spring of 1948)

1949
M-14283 Meadow Green
M-14286 Birch Gray
M-14301 Chrome Yellow
M-1722 Vermilion
M-1724 Medium Luster Black

1950
M-14197 Silvertone Gray
M-14283 Meadow Green
M-14285 Sheridan Blue
M-14341 Palisade Green
M-1722 Vermilion
M-1724 Black

1951
A. Black
B. Sheridan Blue
D. Alpine Blue
G. Sea Island Green
H. Silvertone Gray
M. Meadow Green
N. Vermilion

1952
Black
Sheridan
Blue
Alpine Blue
Woodsmoke
Gray
Shannon Green
Meadowbrook Green
Glenmist Green

Carnival Red
Hawaiian Bronze
Sandpiper Tan

1953
Raven Black
Sheridan Blue
Glacier Blue
Light Green
Vermilion
Meadow Green
Dovetone Gray

1954
Raven Black
Sheridan Blue
Glacier Blue
Light Green
Vermilion
Meadow Green
Goldenrod Yellow

1955
Raven Black
Banner Blue
Aquatone Blue
Waterfall Blue
Snowshoe White
Sea Sprite Green
Vermilion
Meadow Green
Goldenrod Yellow

1956
A. Raven Black
B. Diamond Blue
D. Nocturne Blue
E. Colonial White (for two-tones)
G. Meadowmist Green
H. Platinum Gray
P. Primer Gray
R. Vermilion
S. Special color order
U. Meadow Green
V. Goldenrod Yellow

Appendix B: Rating Plates and How to Read the Serial Numbers

1948-50 Identification Information

Ford identified the year built, model, engine, plant of origin, and serial number on the vehicle identification number (VIN) located on the clutch-plate housing.

The first character indicates the year
   8 = 1948
   9 = Both 1949 and 1950

The second and third characters show engine series

1948 models
   8HC =1948 six-cylinder
   F-18RC =1948 V-8
   F-18HD =1948 six-cylinder
   F-28RD =1948 V-8
   F-28HY =1948 six-cylinder
   F-38RY =1948 V-8

1949 models
   9HC =1949 six-cylinder
   F-19RC =1949 V-8
   F-19HD =1949 six-cylinder
   F-29RD =1949 V-8
   F-29HY =1949 six-cylinder
   F-39RY =1949 V-8

1950 models
   9HC =1950 six-cylinder
   F-19RC =1950 V-8
   F-19HD =1950 six-cylinder
   F-29RD =1950 V-8
   F-29HY =1950 six-cylinderF-39RY =1950 V-8

The last series is the production number for the engine, not the vehicle, from a specific plant.

The body number on the cab is not the same as the VIN.

Note: serial numbers for 1950 models started at 92251 (six-cylinder) and 73088 (V-8)

1951-52 Rating Plates

The rating plate, located in the drop-down door of the glovebox, identified the model, engine, year built, assembly plant produced in, the style of body, and the production number for that vehicle. The VIN number was also located on the clutch housing and engine block. Below are the identification keys for the rating plate.

The first two characters indicate the model of truck
   F1 F2 F3

The third character indicates the engine type
   D = 215 L-head six-cylinder
   R = 239 L-head V-8
   M = 254 L-head six-cylinder
   J = 279 L-head V-8
   K = 317 L-head V-8

The fourth is a number and indicates the year in which the truck was built
   1 = 1951
   2 = 1952

The fifth and sixth characters indicate the plant where the vehicle was built
   AT = Atlanta, Georgia
   BF = Buffalo, New York
   CH = Chicago, Illinois
   CS = Chester, Pennsylvania
   DS = Dallas, Texas
   EG = Edgewater, New Jersey
   HM = Highland Park, Michigan
   KC = Kansas City, Missouri
   LB = Long Beach, California
   LU = Louisville, Kentucky
   MP = Memphis, Tennessee
   NR = Norfolk, Virginia
   RH = Richmond, California
   SP = Twin Cities, Minnesota (St. Paul)
   SR = Somerville, Massachusetts

The last characters identify the production number of that vehicle in a specific plant. All vehicles for 1951-1952 began with 100001, so as many as 16 trucks in any given year could have the same serial number, but with a different assembly plant code on the Rating Plate.

1953-56 Rating Plates

The first three characters indicate the model of truck
   F10 = F-100
   F25 = F-250
   F35 = F-350

The next character indicates the engine type
   D = 215 OHV six-cylinder (1953)
   R = 239 L-head V-8 (1953)
   D = 223 OHV six-cylinder (1954)
   V = 239 OHV V-8 (1954)
   D = 223 OHV six-cylinder (1955)
   U = 239 OHV V-8 (1955)
   D = 223 OHV six-cylinder (1956)
   U = 272 OHV V-8 (1956)

The next is a number that indicates the year the truck was built
   3 = 1953

4 = 1954
5 = 1955
6 = 1956

The next character, a letter, indicates the plant where the vehicle was built

A = Atlanta, Georgia
B = Buffalo, New York
C = Chester, Pennsylvania
D = Dallas, Texas
E = Edgewater, New Jersey (1948-54)
    Mahwah, New Jersey (1955-56)
F = Dearborn, Michigan
H = Highland Park, Michigan
G = Chicago, Illinois
K = Kansas City, Missouri
L = Long Beach, California
M = Memphis, Tennessee
N = Norfolk, Virginia
P = Twin Cities, Minnesota (St. Paul)
R = Richmond, California
S = Somerville, Massachusetts
U = Louisville, Kentucky

The last series of numbers is the sequence in which the vehicle was built at that plant

AT = Atlanta, Georgia
BF = Buffalo, New York
CS = Chester, Pennsylvania
DL = Dallas, Texas
DA = Dearborn, Michigan
EG = Edgewater, New Jersey (1948-54)
HM = Highland Park, Michigan
CH = Chicago, Illinois
KC = Kansas City, Missouri
LB = Long Beach, California
MP = Memphis, Tennessee
NR = Norfolk, Virginia
SP = Twin Cities, Minnesota (St. Paul)
RH = Richmond, California (closed Feb. 1955)
SR = Somerville, Mass.
LU = Louisville, Kentucky
    Windsor, Ontario, Canada (closed July 1954)

Richmond, California - Opened July 10, 1930. Closed and moved operations to San Jose, Calif., Feb. 24, 1955.
Edgewater, New Jersey - Closed in 1954 and moved operations to Mahwah, New Jersey, same year.
Windsor, Canada - Closed in July 1954 and moved operations to Oakville, Ontario, in August same year.

Appendix C: Sales Figures

Light Truck sales - 1948-56
Year-By-Year Sales - Ford Versus the Competition
(no medium or heavy trucks included in totals)

Year	Ford	Chevy	Dodge	Int'l
1948	181,043	229,463	71,785	85,055
1949	165,340	296,001	85,314	46,825
1950	254,144	344,532	77,924	49,840
1951	191,296	282,760	82,521	50,647
1952	124,819	212,578	76,121	47,877
1953	204,806	268,252	62,232	52,583
1954	201,240	230,223	42,950	45,107
1955	218,231	256,327	47,929	48,132
1956	184,154	237,412	43,139	49,483

Appendix D: Year-By-Year Ford F-Series Changes

1948

The early model grille housings were painted Tucson tan (Argent gray later in the model run) and the grilles were Argent gray.
Late 1948 models also had red pinstriping on the grilles.
A chrome grille was a $10 option and wheels came in black.
Argent paint, which is a light silvery-gray, was used on many trim parts during the first few years of F-Series production.
The wing-vent frames were chrome.
The pickup bed was a carry-over from the 1947 model.
The cab was the big change with more room and comfort promoted in the "Bonus Built" advertising theme.
Base prices on F-1 models:
F-1 six-cylinder $1,212
F-1 V-8 $1,239

1949

Wheels were now matched to the body color.
Grilles and grille housing were Argent gray, but without the red pinstriping.
In keeping with using less chrome to support the Korean War efforts, much of the chrome was dropped.
Wing-vent frames, outside mirror, front bumper (and optional rear), gas cap and filler neck, and running boards were all standard in black.
Base prices on F-1 models:
F-1 six-cylinder $1,250

1950

The grille recess was finished in an ivory color.
Grilles continued in either Argent gray or optional chrome finish.
The F-1 badges on the side of the hood were now stamped stainless steel.
Base prices on F-1:
$1,175

1951
An all-new bullet-style grille was introduced, giving the F-1 a new look.

During the first part of the production run, the trucks came with Argent gray grilles and chrome headlamp surrounds. Later, the grille was changed to an ivory color and the chrome around the lamps was changed to Argent.

Dual wipers were now standard.

The 5-Star cab came standard with horsehair seat cushions. The 5-Star Extra cab came with foam cushions.

The easiest way to identify a 1951 model was by the nose of the hood.

The word FORD was stamped into the chrome piece on the hood.

Base prices on F-1 models:
F-1 six-cylinder $1,250

1952
The nose vent on the front of the hood was now painted.

Block letters spelled out FORD just below the hood nose and above the grille opening, similar to the 1948-50 models.

A small red circle with the F-designation was added to the front of the arrow emblems on the sides of the hood.

Hubcaps now came in silver, not chrome.

The three-speed column-shift transmission was now standard on the F-1 models.

The 1952 models were uniquely badged with block FORD letters above the grille and under the nose of the hood.

Base prices on F-1 models:
F-1 six-cylinder $1,329

1953
The first of the all-new bodies since the 1948 F-Series.

The front axle was moved back approximately 4 inches, providing a shorter turning radius than previous models.

This was the first usage of the new Ford truck crest emblem, located on the front hood nose.

The same flathead V-8 was carried over from the previous models, but a new 115-horsepower overhead-valve six-cylinder engine replaced the old model.

The pickup beds were made of interlocked hardwood with steel runners for protection.

The horizontal grille came in two versions: one with chrome "teeth" on either side of center (Deluxe) and one without (Standard).

Base prices on F-100 models:
F-100 six-cylinder $1,012

1954
These models came with a new grille, much bulkier, less streamlined than the 1953 trucks.

New overhead-valve "Y-block" V-8 engines were added for the first time.

The grille was rather unsightly, large, and bulky. It came with chrome sergeant stripes on either side of the V-8 emblem.

Base prices on F-100 models:
F-100 six-cylinder $1,292

1955
Grilles continued to be an easy, economical visual change.

The 1955 model had a large "V" in the center of the grille (cut in from the top) and contained an emblem designating the engine.

A four-star emblem designated a six-cylinder and an "8" identified it as V-8 power.

Custom Cab models replaced the Deluxe cab.

Base prices on F-100 models:
F-100 six-cylinder $1,382

1956
The first year for the wraparound front windshield and push-button door handles.

Optional larger rear window.

Although the basic styling was carried over, there were major changes to the cab.

The advertising campaigns focused on a "Driverized" cab.

Woven-plastic seat covers replaced vinyl.

Safety features such as the Life-Guard deep-dish steering wheel were also added.

Along with Colonial White, basic paint offerings could be combined for two-tone paint scheme.

Tubeless tires were standard.

The grille style this year moved back to something more similar to the 1953 grille.

These models had two horizontal bars, smooth on the top with a "V" dropping out of the bottom of the top bar. The top bar was larger than the bottom one.

Base prices on F-100 models:
F-100 six-cylinder $1,485

Base prices (Canadian currency)
Canadian Ford and Mercury model trucks:

Year	Ford F-47 pickup	Mercury M-47 pickup
1948	$1,398	$1,435
1949	$1,572	$1,641
1950	$1,524	$1,542
1951	$1,663	$1,663
1952	$1,745	$1,745

Year	Ford F-100 pickup	Mercury F-100 pickup
1953	$1,748	$1,749
1954	$1,749	$1,749
1955	$1,782	$1,782
1956	$1,971	$1,971

Note: All 1948-56 model Canadian trucks came standard with a 239 V-8 engine.